AF511875

Islam for Hindus

Islam for Hindus

Arvind Sharma

D.K. Printworld (P) Ltd.
New Delhi

Cataloging in Publication Data — DK

[Courtesy: D.K. Agencies (P) Ltd. <docinfo@dkagencies.com>]

Sharma, Arvind, 1940-

Islam for Hindus / Arvind Sharma.

p. cm.

Includes bibliographical references.

ISBN 13: 9788124605165

ISBN 10: 8124605165

1. Islam. 2. Islam — Relations — Hinduism.
3. Hinduism — Relations — Islam. I. Title.

DDC 294.284 5 22

© Arvind Sharma

First published in India, 2009

ISBN 13: 978-81-246-0516-5 (Pb) ISBN 10: 81-246-0516-5

All rights reserved. No part of this publication may be reproduced or transmitted in any form or by any means, electronic or mechanical, including photocopying, recording, or any information storage or retrieval system, without prior written permission of both the copyright holder and the publishers.

Published and printed by:

D.K. Printworld (P) Ltd.

Regd. office : *'Srikunj,'* F-52, Bali Nagar

Ramesh Nagar Metro Station

New Delhi – 110 015

Phones : (011) 2545 3975; 2546 6019; *Fax* : (011) 2546 5926

E-mail: dkprintworld@vsnl.net

Web: www.dkprintworld.com

Contents

Introduction

This book aims to provide basic knowledge about Islam to Hindus. Such a book, however, could achieve its goal in many different ways. I would therefore like to explain to the reader the reasons underlying the form it has assumed, before the reader embarks on its study.

The interaction between Hinduism and Islam on the Indian subcontinent has often, though not always, been a vexed one in many ways. The two religions have therefore tended to view each other through such a lens. This has meant that the understanding each has of the other is often emotionally charged, and that charge has been often negative. And because of this emotional overload, the knowledge each religious tradition possesses of the other has tended to be judgemental rather than factual. With this in mind, this book is an attempt to provide a *factual* introduction to Islam *in general*. I use the expression "in general" advisedly, as this is not a book about Islam in India, although it is in India that ninety-five per cent of the Hindus of the world reside. It is intended to introduce the Hindu reader to Islam in general, under such rubrics as the concept of the prophet, the life of the Prophet Muḥammad, the Qur'ān, the Pillars of Islam, Islamic Law, the history of Islam, and Islamic mysticism. A final chapter focuses on the question: Can Muslims talk to Hindus?

Readers might well wonder why Islam has been presented here in such a decontextualized way, in a manner one might find it presented in a book on world religions, rather than as it might be presented in a book on the religions of India, or in a book on Indian history. There is a reason underlying this mode of presentation and that reason is that one factor, which often complicates the interaction between these two religions, is sheer mutual ignorance. Most Hindus in India do not seem to know much about Islam, as a religious tradition, on its own, just as Muslims in India probably do not know much about the Hindu religious tradition on its own. Each religion rather knows the other as it has historically encountered it. The historical issues, arising out of this encounter, have moulded the mutual perception of these traditions to such an extent that it almost seems to require an act of intellectual will to be able to see these religious traditions as a whole, each in its *own* context.

This book is therefore an attempt to go beyond — or to transcend, if you will — such mutual historical conditioning. It is not the implication of such a "non-historical" approach that history is not important, or that historical issues, which have arisen as a result of the encounter between the two traditions, may be pushed under the carpet and not be looked in the face. Far from it. The belief underlying such a book, however, is that the understanding of a tradition generated by an encounter with it may not tell us all that is worth knowing about it. After all, if we know a tradition only in terms of our encounter with it, then we know it only in terms of that encounter, and not as a whole. The holistic knowledge gained through the kind of exercise represented by the book, which presents a tradition outside the context in which it was encountered, may also allow us to form a more nuanced judgement about the nature of our historical encounter with it. It may also enable us to respond to the historical issues, which may have arisen out of the historical encounter, in ways which may not otherwise be possible. It is true that this distinction between the "history" of a religion and its "nature," as it were, has its limits and can be overdone, but this distinction seems to have been hardly invoked in the present context.

I have therefore taken the liberty of offering here a historically aseptic presentation of Islam so far as the Indian subcontinent is concerned, and also of directing attention to those elements of the Hindu tradition which might provide a parallel to the aspect of Islam under study, when the two traditions are viewed as independent religious systems. These comparisons are, however, highly tentative in nature and are offered as suggestions rather than conclusions, for I would like to emphasize that one might, before offering them as conclusions, wish to acquaint oneself with the religious traditions as a whole, as fully as possible, a condition I cannot claim to meet in the present state of my knowledge or ignorance.

Allow me, however, to offer two examples of how studying the two traditions on their own turfs as it were, might enhance our understanding of these traditions, before one takes on the more delicate task of instituting comparisons between the two as I might have rashly done. Both these examples are potentially contentious but I have chosen them deliberately to compensate, as it were, for the straightforward nature of the account which is to follow.

The aspect of Hinduism which Muslims recognize immediately, speaking historically, is its hierarchical social structure, often associated with the word *jāti*. When viewed in a holistic perspective, however, it might be susceptible to a more mellowed understanding. Many observers of the Indian scene, beginning with the earliest, both indigenous and foreign, remark on the plurality and diversity which characterizes what we now call Hinduism from its very inception, whenever we might locate it. The existence of such plurality and diversity immediately creates the problem of managing it. In other words, the main problem which Hinduism has had to grapple with, as a religious system in the face of the bewildering variety it plays host to, is order. Now one of the simplest, and also perhaps the most common way, of achieving order is hierarchy, as an antidote to anarchy. Could this not explain Hinduism's tendency to hierarchize? This also sheds light on the question of justice within Hinduism, in the context of the inegalitarianism which often accompanies such hierarchy, especially when it gets frozen. It is not that Hinduism is indifferent to justice; what complicates the situation is the fact that while order without justice is possible, justice without order is impossible. So before Hinduism can turn to justice, it must tackle the question of order. If this fact is kept in mind, then the proclivity to hierarchy within Hinduism can be viewed as a systemic rather than an arbitrary or perverse phenomenon. This again does not mean that the problems this need for order creates should or can be ignored or overlooked; what such a holistic view does is to enhance our appreciation of the issue in a way as might facilitate its resolution.

An aspect of Islam which Hindus recognize immediately, speaking historically, is militancy, often associated with the word *jihād*. When viewed from a holistic perspective, however, it too might be susceptible to a more mellowed understanding. In the case of some religions, state-formation is *not* simultaneous with their appearance. Hinduism itself had many years, indeed centuries, of existence behind it, before the Mauryans (preceded by the Nandas) set about establishing the first Indian historical empire in India in fourth century BCE. Even earlier, the clear differentiation between the roles of the *brāhmaṇa* and the *kṣatriya* may have militated against the kind of centralization required for state and empire building. The case of Christianity is even less ambiguous. Not only does Jesus famously ask one to render unto Caesar what is Caesar's and God what is God's, the Roman state in fact was first opposed to Christianity, before the relationship got reversed under Constantine. The Roman state ran parallel to Christianity rather than Christianity coinciding with its emergence, and Christianity gained access to political power centuries after its appearance as a religion. In the case of Islam, however, the emergence of the state in Arabia was coeval with the emergence of Islam. It may not be inappropriate to invoke the metaphor of Siamese twins in this context at this point, if it is insisted upon that other religions may also have enjoyed a symbiotic relationship with the state at times. Now according to most anthropologists and historians, state formation, whether it be in small scale or large scale societies, is hardly ever a pretty affair, and often a sanguinary one. If this is kept in mind, then the problems that might be caused by such a fusion of religion and politics in Islam begin to appear as something systemic and not arbitrary or perverse. This does not mean that the problems such as intimate association gives rise to may be ignored or overlooked, but what it does mean is that one can now take an analytical as distinguished from a stereotypical view of the matter. Such an approach, in one sense analytical and in another holistic, enhances our appreciation of the situation in such a way as might be more conducive to the resolution of the issues created by the fact of the natal intimacy of state and religion in Islam.

It is my hope, nurtured by the spirit which animates these two examples, that the portrait of Islam, as presented in the pages that follow, will contribute to a more nuanced and holistic understanding of Islam as a religious phenomenon on the part of the reader. I would also like the readers to draw my attention to any errors that may have crept into my account of Islam, as my interest in the subject far exceeds my knowledge of it.

1

The Concept of a Prophet

ONE way to begin to get an idea of what Islam is all about is to realize that Islam belongs to a family of religions, now usually referred to as the Abrahamic religions, because all three of them acknowledge Abraham as part of their history. These are the three religions of Judaism, Christianity and Islam. This Abrahamic family of religions is comparable, as a family of religions, to what has been called the Indic family of religions, or Indic religions, for short. This term is applied as a common rubric to the religions which arose in India, namely, Hinduism, Buddhism, Jainism and Sikhism. This parallel is helpful in several ways. Just as the religions of Hinduism, Buddhism, Jainism and Sikhism arose in India, the three members of the Abrahamic family — Judaism, Christianity and Islam, arose in the Near East. And just as the four religions of Indian origin share certain key concepts, such as those of *karma* and rebirth for instance, although their precise connotation within them might vary, similarly the three religions of Judaism, Christianity and Islam share certain key concepts such as those of God, heaven and hell, and prophets.

One may be tempted to ask at this stage: If the various members of the Abrahamic religious tradition share certain features in common and the various members of the Indic religious tradition also share certain features in common, do these two families of religions also share certain features in common? Religions belonging to both these families possess their own scriptures, systems of ethics, places of pilgrimage and so on but for the present purpose of understanding the nature of Islam as a religion, it is not so much their similarity as a point of difference which acquires special significance, specially when we narrow our focus to Hinduism among the religions of Indian origin.

This consists of the fact that Hinduism, when understood as a religion in the Western sense of the word, has no historical founder. Christianity can be traced back to Christ and Islam can be traced back to Prophet Muḥammad, but Hinduism cannot be traced back to any such individual. The best one can do in this regard is to say that perhaps the *ṛṣis* could be looked upon in some sense as the founders of Hinduism. The Vedas are considered to be the foundational texts of Hinduism and these were revealed to the *ṛṣis*. In this sense then the *ṛṣis* could be considered the founders of Hinduism.

It will be obvious to the reader that the point is being forced and this should provide us with a major clue when it comes to gaining an understanding of the Abrahamic religious tradition in general and Islam in particular — that they are "historical" religions in the sense that history possesses a *religious* significance in the context of these religious traditions which is not paralleled in Hinduism. And this difference is highlighted by the fact that while Hinduism does not even seem to possess a historical founder, the Abrahamic religions contain clear-cut accounts of the historical circumstances in which they arose.

There is a particular type of a person connected with their emergence, just as a particular type of human beings, called the seers or *ṛṣis* are connected with the emergence of Hinduism. However, whereas in Hinduism the seers constitute a collectivity in general, in which their chronological order is of little special significance, the historical order in which the *prophets* appear is specially significant in the case of the Abrahamic religions. But before we proceed any further we need to know what is meant by this class of people called the prophets. Huston Smith explains the term as follows:

> When someone today is referred to as a prophet or is said to prophesy, we think of a soothsayer — someone who foretells the future. This was not the original meaning of the word. "Prophet" comes from the Greek word *prophetes*, in which *pro* means "for" and *phetes* means "to speak." Thus, in its original Greek, a prophet is someone who "speaks for" someone else. This meaning is faithful to the original Hebrew. When God commissions Moses to demand from Pharaoh the release of his people and Moses protests that he cannot speak, God says, "Your brother Aaron shall be your prophet" (Exodus 7:1).
>
> If for the Hebrews the generic meaning of the word prophet was "one who speaks on the authority of another," its specific meaning (as used to refer to a distinctive group of people in the biblical period) was "one who speaks for God." A prophet differed from other men in that his mind, his speech, and occasionally

> even his body could become a conduit through which God addressed immediate historical conditions.[1]

The prophet then is a person who speaks for God.

The historical setting for the emergence of prophecy is one which, in broad details, is shared by the Abrahamic religions. These details go as follows. The story begins with

> God's creation of heaven and earth and of man. Man, however, dissatisfied with his position of subjection to God within the created order, rebelled against his Maker. God's method of dealing with this situation was to choose one man, Abraham, out of all the fallen mass of mankind, whose descendants were to form a nucleus of faithful people, and to be both the recipients of the divine blessing and the source of its mediation to all men.[2]

One can now see why the description of Judaism, Christianity and Islam as Abrahamic religions stands justified. Abraham, whom modern scholars of religion assign to *c.* 1800 BCE, is the founder of Judaism, in whose shaping Moses, usually assigned to *c.* 1250 BCE, was also to play a major role.

The account of the creation of the world, the first human being, and the circumstances which lead to the fallenness of human beings differs in detail in Judaism, Christianity

---

1. Huston Smith, *The World's Religions* (San Francisco: Harper Collins, 1991), p. 288.
2. J.G. Davies, "Christianity: The Early Church", in R.C. Zaehner, ed., *The Concise Encyclopedia of Living Faiths* (Boston: Beacon Press, 1967), p. 51. Abbreviated.

and Islam. Since this book is concerned with Islam we present the following account which follows the Islamic perspective:

> Adam, a figure known from the Hebrew Bible, is the father of humankind. He is the first sinner; his sin is his violation of the principle of submission (*islām*) to God, through disobedience. The story of Adam in the Qur'ān shows humankind's proclivity to evil. Yet God fashions this sinful earthly creature with his own two hands and breathes into him his spirit. (For the story of Adam in the Qur'ān, see *sūrah* 7:12-26 and 20:114-27. But for a major difference from the *Genesis* account of Adam's creation and fall, see 2:30-39).
>
> But Adam is also the first prophet. Before he and his spouse disobey God and eat of the forbidden tree, "God taught Adam all the names" (Qur'ān. 2:31). With this revelation to his earthly creature, God challenges the angels. This is because they have protested against God's choosing such an insignificant creature and his potentially wicked progeny to be his stewards on earth. God orders the protesting angels to bow down reverently before him. They all do, except Satan, who is also called in Arabic Iblīs (many consider the name's resemblance to Greek *diabolos*, coincidental). Satan arrogantly refuses to bow down before a creature of clay, while he himself has been created of fire and thus thinks himself to be better than Adam. Because of this sin of arrogant rebellion, Satan is expelled by God from the company of the angels. He is allowed, however, to tempt Adam and the weak among his descendants into disobeying God till the day of Resurrection.

> After Adam and Eve, and by implication the rest of humankind, are expelled from the garden, God promises them salvation through revelation: "There shall come from me to you [humankind] guidance, and whoever follows my guidance, no fear shall come upon them, nor will they grieve" (Qur'ān 2:38).[3]

This expulsion of Adam may be familiar to Indian readers through its invocation in Urdu poetry. Two of the leading Urdu poets of the Indian subcontinent have alluded to it each in his own inimitable way. Mirzā Ghālib refers to it in his famous couplet as follows:

> *nikalanā khuld se ādam kā sunate āye the lekin* ।
> *baḍe be-ābarū hokar tere kūce se ham nikale* ॥

Allama Iqbal, writing almost a century later, again refers to it as follows:

> *bāge-bahisht se muzhe iznesafar diyā thā kyon* ।
> *karejahān darāz hai ab merā intazār kar* ॥

But I digress!

The understanding of prophecy in Islam also has its special feature which is apparent in the following statement about it:

> According to the Qur'ān and Islamic tradition, God's role in human history is not played by him directly through self-disclosure or incarnation in a divine human being, as Christians affirm of Jesus. Rather, God operates through his prophets and messengers, who

---

3. Mahmoud M. Ayoub, "The Islamic Tradition", in Willard G. Oxtoby, ed., *World Religions: Western Traditions* (Toronto: Oxford University Press, 1996), p. 363.

> convey his will in revealed scriptures and seek to establish his sacred law in the lives of their communities. From the Islamic point of view, therefore, human history is prophetic history.[4]

Abraham appeared in the course of this prophetic history and laid the foundations of Judaism *c.* 1800 BCE. Jesus appeared in the course of this prophetic history and laid the foundations of Christianity *c.* 4 BCE and Muḥammad appeared in the sixth century and laid the foundations of Islam.

Before we turn to an examination of his life it might be worth noting that the concept of prophets in the Abrahamic religious tradition is analogous to that of the *avatāra*s or incarnations in Hinduism. God does not incarnate Himself in the Abrahamic religious tradition except in the case of Christianity. The idea of God incarnating Himself is so unusual in that tradition that Christianity is criticized both in Judaism and Islam for adopting such a position. The two ideas are however comparable in significant ways. Just as a number of prophets have appeared in a particular order in the Abrahamic religious tradition, a number of the incarnations of God, specially Viṣṇu, are recorded in the Hindu tradition. And just as the prophets often arise in a context in which justice has to be asserted in the face of oppression, the justification for the appearance of incarnations within Hinduism is offered in similar terms in a famous verse of the *Bhagavad-Gītā* (IV.8). It is perhaps this similarity between the two which explains the fact that when Mahmūd of Ghazna had the Islamic confession of

4. Mahmoud M. Ayoub, op. cit., p. 363.

faith embossed on his coins in Sanskrit, Prophet Muḥammad was referred to as an *avatāra*. The translation of the entire *shahādah* ran as follows: *avyaktam ekam muḥammad avatāraḥ*. Such a description is problematical in strictly theological terms, which makes this historical fact all the more piquant. Further evidence of this is provided by the following remark, made by a well-known scholar of religion: "I had been searching in the wrong places and looking in the wrong way. I thought Muhammad was a kind of *avatāra*, somewhat like Jesus or the Buddha, but he is not that kind of incarnation. In fact Islam does have an *avatāra*: The Qur'ān itself."[5]

5. Huston Smith (with Jeffry Paine), *Tales of Wonder : Huston Smith — An Autobiography*, New York: Harper Collins, 2009, p. 146.

2

The Life of Prophet Muḥammad

IT IS necessary to form some idea of the Arabia of his times in order to appreciate the life and prophetic role of Prophet Muḥammad. Arabia at the time was inhabited by a number of tribes who were in a constant state of conflict with each other. The concept of tribal honour played an important role in these conflicts, as a tribe was honour-bound to avenge the death of any of its members at the hands of another, and sometimes the effort was spread over generations. The ghost of the slain person was supposed to hover around until such revenge was exacted. At the same time, the virtues of hospitality and martial courage were much prized. These tribes held the precincts of the shrine of Ka'bah as sacred "where no living thing — plant, animal, or human — could be harmed. For Makkah (Mecca) and most of Arabia, the chief *haram* [sacred place] was the Shrine of Ka'bah and its environs. It was believed to have been built by Abraham and his son Ishmael, brought by Abraham and his mother, Hagar, to settle in the valley of Makkah."[1] In other words, Ka'bah was like a *tīrtha-sthāna*

---

1. Mahmoud M. Ayoub, op. cit., p. 355. The Islamic and Judeo-Christian accounts diverge in this respect. The following general account provided by Huston Smith is helpful in clarifying the overall context (op. cit., pp. 222-23):

→

where no warfare could be carried out. A fair was also held during the pilgrimage season at this site.

The Arabs of those days did not believe in an after-life and:

> believed time to be synonymous with death or fate, which in the end will spare no one. Therefore, while a person can, he or she should make the most of this life. Arab society was thus largely given to hedonistic pleasures, finding no other meaning in existence. The Qur'ān describes this attitude as gloomy: "They (the Arabs) say there is only this life of ours; we live and

---

→ God created the world, and after it human beings. The name of the first man was Adam. The descendants of Adam led to Noah, who had a son named Shem. This is where the word Semite comes from; literally a Semite is a descendant of Shem. Like the Jews, the Arabs consider themselves a Semitic people. The descendants of Shem led to Abraham, and so far we are still in the tradition of Judaism and Christianity. Indeed, it was the submission of Abraham in his supreme test — would he be willing to sacrifice his son Ishmael? — that appears to have provided Islam with its name. Abraham married Sarah. Sarah had no son, so Abraham, wanting to continue his line, took Hagar for his second wife. Hagar bore him a son, Ishmael, whereupon Sarah conceived and likewise had a son, named Isaac. Sarah then demanded that Abraham banish Ishmael and Hagar from the tribe. Here we come to the first divergence between the Koranic and biblical accounts. According to the Koran, Ishmael went to the place where Mecca was to rise. His descendants, flourishing in Arabia, became Muslims; whereas those of Isaac, who remained in Palestine, were Hebrews and became Jews.

> we die, and time alone will destroy us all" (Qur'ān 45:24). These sentiments were expressed in eloquent odes recounting deeds of chivalry and generosity, deploring fate, and praising the wise man who drowns his sorrows in the pleasures of wine, women, and sentimental verse, but is sure to leave behind a good name for his tribe to boast of after him.[2]

The existence of two classes of people in this society is noteworthy: *kāhin*s and *ḥanīf*s. *Kāhin*s were sooth-sayers. "Such a man or woman spoke in rhyme and mysterious phrases that were meant to announce an important event, answer a perplexing question, or evoke fear and wonderment among the *kāhin*'s listeners."[3] By contrast, *ḥanīf*s were believers in one true God — or Arab monotheists, as distinguished from Jewish and Christian monotheists. Both these religious traditions were known to the Arabs and specially Meccans, for Mecca fell on the trade route between the East and the West.

The pre-Islamic state of Arabia came to be looked upon as one of *jāhilīyah* (foolishness or ignorance) after the emergence of Islam, a semantic resonance still heard in the use of the word *jāhil* to chastize the inadvertent and the ignorant.

One particular feature of Arab society must be noted. The Qur'ān hints at the expectation among the Arabs that just as the Jews and the Christians had received revelations

---

2. Mahmoud M. Ayoub, op. cit., p. 356.
3. Ibid., p. 358.

from God, perhaps the Arabs will also become the recipients of one.[4]

Muḥammad was born around the year 570 in the tribe of Quraysh. It is an interesting fact that while the date of his birth is not known, unlike that of Jesus Christ which is celebrated throughout the Christian world, it is the first reception of the revelation which came to be known as the Qur'ān by him, which is celebrated in the Islamic world with the same éclat.[5] His father died before he was born, while away on a caravan journey and his mother died a few years after his birth. Muḥammad was thus orphaned in early life and brought up by his paternal grandfather, 'Abd al-Muṭṭalib. The grandfather passed away while Muḥammad was still a youth, when he was taken under the wing by his uncle Abū Ṭālib. Not much is mentioned of his early youth even in the earliest biography of the Prophet,[6]

---

4. Mahmoud M. Ayoub, op. cit., pp. 356-57.
5. The point should however not be exaggerated. The exact date of the birth of Jesus is far from certain according to scholars, although the 25th of December is celebrated as such in the Christian world. Similarly, although the date of birth of the Prophet is not known for certain according to scholars, devout Muslims believe the date to be the 17th of Rabi Al-Awwal, 570 of the Islamic calendar and this birthday or *mawlid* is celebrated by many Muslims. It is the *relative* weight attached to the birth of Jesus and the reception of the Qur'ān in the two traditions which constitutes the point of comparison here.
6. See A. Guillaume, *The Life of Muhammad: A Translation of Ishaq's sīrat rasūl allāh* (Karachi: Oxford University Press, 1980 [1955]) *passim*.

but we know that he had the reputation of being extremely trustworthy by the fact that he was called *al-amīn* (or the trustworthy one), just as someone very honest may be called *satyavān* in Hindu circles.

We encounter him in his youth in the service of a wealthy widow named Khadījah, on whose behalf he would conduct business. The association deepened into affection despite the difference in age between the two — she is believed to have been 40 and he was 25. She proposed marriage. He accepted and began to lead the life of a well-to-do merchant of Mecca.

It is surely not on this account that his name lays a claim on our attention today. For that, one has to turn to another dimension of his life — the spiritual. Muḥammad possessed a contemplative disposition, which led him to spend time in silent meditation in a cave on the mountain Hirā' in the vicinity of Mecca, specially in the month of Ramaḍān.

One night, while he thus sat locked in meditation, he heard a heavenly voice calling upon him to recite. Upon asking what he should recite he was told:

> Recite, in the name of thy lord who created
> Created man from a clot!
> Recite, for thy lord is the Most Bountiful
> Who taught by the pen,
> Taught man what he knew not![7]

This is the first revelation received by prophet Muḥammad according to Tradition. It is worth sharing a fuller account of this event as provided by Pickthall, whose English

---

7. H.A.R. Gibb, "Islam," in R.C. Zaehner, op. cit., p. 179.

translation of the Qur'ān is widely used. After noting that Muḥammad used to retire to Mount Hirā' to meditate, he writes:

> It was there one night toward the end of his quiet month that the first revelation came to him when he was forty years old. He was asleep or in a trance when he heard a voice say: "Read!" He said: "I cannot read." A third time the voice, more terrible, commanded: "Read!" He said: "What can I read?" The voice said:
>
> Read: In the name of thy Lord Who createth.
> Createth man from a clot.
> Read: And it is thy Lord the Most Bountiful
> Who teacheth by the pen,
> Teacheth man that which he knew not.
>
> When he awoke the words remained "as if inscribed upon his heart." He went out of the cave on to the hillside and heard the same awe-inspiring voice say: "O Muhammad! Thou art Allah's messenger, and I am Gabriel." Then he raised his eyes and saw the angel, in the likeness of a man, standing in the sky above the horizon. And again the dreadful voice said: "O Muhammad! Thou art Allah's messenger, and I am Gabriel." Muhammad (God bless and keep him) stood quite still, turning away his face from the brightness of the vision, but whithersoever he might turn his face, there always stood the angel confronting him. He remained thus a long while till at length the angel vanished, when he returned in great distress of mind to his wife Khadījah. She did her best to reassure him, saying that his conduct had been such that Allah would not let a harmful spirit come to him and that it was

> her hope that he was to become the Prophet of his people. On their return to Mecca she took him to her cousin Waraqa ibn Naufal, a very old man, "who knew the Scriptures of the Jews and Christians," who declared his belief that the heavenly messenger who came to Moses of old had come to Muhammad, and that he was chosen as the Prophet of his people.[8]

The role of Khadījah in the confirmation of his role as a prophet is specially worth noting. One of the names of the Prophet literally means the blanket-wearer and this refers to the situation when he appeared before Khadījah shaking under the impact of this experience and she wrapped a mantle around him. Some interpret his being shaken in psychological terms, as the result of this extraordinary experience. Others explain that he was shaking under the weight of the burden God had cast on his shoulders, by making him a prophet to his people. Khadījah stood by him in any case. If it is true that nobody knows a person better than his own wife then we here have the best possible human testimony in the matter. It is also worth noting that in a sense the first convert to Islam was a woman!

As the Prophet received further revelations, he shared them with the Makkans but they were generally not well-received because they contained calls for social justice. After almost a decade of preaching the Prophet had converted several hundred families but also made many enemies among the haves of Makkah. He was however protected

---

8. Mohammed Marmaduke Pickthall, tr., *The Meaning of the Glorious Koran* (New York: The New American Library, 1972), pp. x-xi.

from harm on account of being a protégé of his uncle Abū Ṭālib. His community had been so severely persecuted that a group of them had migrated to Ethiopia, which was a Christian country, where they found refuge.

The turning point came in the year 622. Around this time his uncle, whose prestige had protected him, died, followed by the death of Khadījah herself in less than two months. But a more positive outcome had been in the making for a while. When Arabs made the annual pilgrimage to Makkah they heard of Muḥammad and his teachings. Some of the visitors from the city of Yathrib, situated 250 miles to the north of Makkah, carried the word back home. Now life in Yathrib had been seriously disturbed by tribal rivalries and in 622 the representatives from the city invited Muḥammad to the city to arbitrate their differences, accepting him as a prophet. The city of Yathrib was also re-named as Madīnah or the City (of the Prophet) in his honour. The move however had to be carried out with great circumspection on account of the rivalry between the two cities, the hostility Muḥammad's teaching had provoked and the perception of treachery in his going over to another city.

The move was however successfully accomplished and the Prophet now became the leader of a well-defined community. However, the Muslims of Medina soon came in conflict with the people of Makkah, who had disapproved of the goings-on in the first place. When the Makkan caravans to Syria were intercepted, they sent a detachment of a thousand men which was defeated, in what was to become famous as the Battle of Badr, by a force of 300 Muslims. It was fought in 624 in the month of Ramaḍān and the Prophet attributed the victory to God. The Makkans followed up with another attack the next year. The encounter with the Muslims took place at Uḥud, in which the Muslims did not fare well and the Prophet was himself injured. The Makkans did not press the advantage however, but there was considerable loss of life. The revelation concerning the provision of four wives was received after the battle of Uḥud.

The developments which followed the battle of Uḥud were to prove highly consequential for Muslim-Jewish relations. When the Prophet arrived in Medina it was with the expectation that the Jews would soon join the fold, given the shared belief in monotheism which set both Muslims and Jews apart from the pagan Arabs. At the very least "the Prophet expected the Jews of Medina to recognize his kinship and thus be his natural allies. He adopted a number of Jewish practices, including the fast of the Day of Atonement, Yom Kippur. It seems, moreover, that, as in Jewish usage, the Muslims had from the beginning been facing Jerusalem in their prayers."[9] All this changed within two years, by when the *quiblah* or the direction of prayer was changed to Makkah and the fast in the month of Ramaḍān replaced Yom Kippur. The reason for the change seems to have been the non-acceptance of Muḥammad as a prophet and the Qur'ān as revelation by the Jews. This negative situation was complicated by the battle of Uḥud, during which the Jews were suspected of engaging in treasonable negotiation with the enemy. An arbiter was appointed, who ruled against them. They were offered the

9. Mahmoud M. Ayoub, op. cit., p. 360.

choice between conversion to Islam or death. One person converted, the rest were allowed to say their final prayers and then went to their death.

The Muslims at Medina gradually gained in strength and the Makkans tried to attack them again in 627, deploying cavalry. They were repulsed at the Battle of the Ditch, so called because a ditch had been dug at the advice of a Persian follower of the Prophet to check the cavalry. The truce of Ḥudaybīyah was arranged in 628 by which the Prophet was allowed to visit the Ka'bah. The terms of the truce were however broken and in 630 the Muslims besieged Makkah, and the Makkans surrendered. A general amnesty was granted to all those who embraced Islam. When "the Makkans asked the Prophet what he intended to do with them . . . he answered: 'I will do with you what Joseph did with his brothers. Go; you are free.' Then quoting Joseph's words to his brothers, he continued, 'There is no blame in you today; God forgive you'" (Qur'ān 12:92).[10]

Muḥammad attributed the victory to God.

The Qur'ān refers to this occasion in chapter CX:

> In the Name of Allah, the Beneficent, the Merciful
>
> When Allah's succour and triumph cometh and thou seest mankind entering the religion of Allah in troops, Then hymn the praise of Thy Lord, and seek forgiveness of Him. Lo! He is ever ready to show mercy.[11]

---

10. Mahmoud M. Ayoub, op. cit., p. 362.
11. Seyyed Hossein Nasr, "Islam", in Arvind Sharma, ed., *Our Religions* (San Francisco: Harper Collins, 1993), p. 453.

After the victory, Muḥammad returned to Medina, where he died two years later, in 632. Before his death he undertook the famous farewell pilgrimage to Makkah.

The end came in the form of a headache. When he felt unwell he took permission from all his other wives to rest in 'Ā'ishah's quarters, where he lay down in her care and passed away after being heard to say: "To the company of the blessed ones in heaven." According to tradition, God had offered him a choice between eternal life on earth or the company of the blessed ones in heaven. He had chosen the latter.

Nobody was prepared for the Prophet's death, and some had taken him to be immortal. As one of the earliest biographers of the Prophet, Ibn Ishāq, tells us:

> When the apostle was dead Umar got up and said: "Some of the disaffected will allege that the apostle is dead, but by God he is not dead: he has gone to ḥis Lord as Moses b. Imrān went and was hidden from his people for forty days, returning to them after it was said that he had died. By God, the apostle will return as Moses returned and will cut-off the hands and feet of men who allege that the apostle is dead." When Abū Bakr heard what was happening he came to the door of the mosque as Umar was speaking to the people. He paid no attention but went into Āisha's house to the apostle, who was lying covered by a mantle of Yamanī cloth. He went and uncovered his face and kissed him, saying, "you are dearer than my father and mother. You have tasted the death which God had decreed: a second death will never overtake you." Then he replaced the mantle on the apostle's

> face and went out. Umar was still speaking and he said, gently, "Umar, be quiet." But Umar refused and went on talking, and when Abū Bakr saw that he would not be silent he went forward to the people who, when they heard his words, came to him and left Umar. Giving thanks and praise to God he said: "O men, if anyone worships Muhammad, Muhammad is dead: if anyone worships God, God is alive, immortal." Then he recited this verse: "Muhammad is nothing but an apostle. Apostles have passed away before him. Can it be that if he were to die or be killed you would turn back on your heels? He who turns back does no harm to God and God will reward the grateful." By God, it was as though the people did not know that this verse (Ṭ. concerning the apostle) had come down until Abū Bakr recited it that day. The people took it from him and it was (constantly) in their mouths. Umar said, By God, when I heard Abū Bakr recite these words I was dumbfounded so that my legs would not bear me and I fell to the ground knowing that the apostle was indeed dead.[12]

Abū Bakr was one of the few members of a distinguished family who had sided with the Prophet during the difficult years in Makkah; his daughter was also married to the Prophet. All present offered their fealty to him by grasping his hand.

12. A. Guillaume, op. cit., p. 683. Ṭ stands for Ṭabarī.

3

The Qur'ān

I

THE persistent references to the Qur'ān in the preceding chapters must have already alerted the reader to the central place the Qur'ān occupies in Islam. Before one goes into the matter any further a salient fact must be recognized — that the Qur'ān for a Muslim is *literally* the word of God. This point needs to be emphasized because we are used to having various texts being described as the word of God. The Jewish Torah in some sense is considered the word of God and so is the Bible. When these other scriptures are described as the word of God, however, they are often understood in a metaphorical or symbolical sense and if we were to understand the Qur'ān too as the word of God in this sense then we would miss the point. For the Muslim the Qur'ān is *literally* the word of God.

This point cannot be overemphasized. One may convey some of its force by referring to two aspects of Islam which will help underscore this point. There is a strong tradition within Islam that the Prophet was non-literate — in the sense that he could not read or write. It might appear strange to us, especially if one is familiar with Western ways of doing business, that someone could function as a businessman without knowing how to read or write. The case might have appeared less incredible to people of an earlier generation, when the rate of literacy in India was much lower than it is now. In that earlier age it was possible to meet people in person in India who were immensely rich and successful businessmen, but who could not read or write. Thus the claim that prophet Muḥammad could not read or write, although a successful businessman, cannot be dismissed although it strains our credulity somewhat.

However, to think of the matter in this light is to completely miss the point. Scholars of religion have argued that the Prophet is considered "unlettered" to indicate that when God's words passed through him and became human words, he did not in any way mix any of his *own* words with them. An educated man may find the temptation to editorialise even God's words difficult to resist, but in the case of the Prophet there was no such temptation at work. In this respect, the idea of the "illiteracy" of the Prophet has often been compared to the virginity of Mary in the context of Jesus' birth. The channel of God's communication in Islam is the word of God; the channel in the case of Christianity is the person of Jesus, Word which had become flesh. And both traditions seem anxious to pre-empt the charge that the process of the reception of revelation may have adulterated the product in any way. This is one way in which the idea that the Qur'ān is literally the word of God is safeguarded. The second point which supports this view is the distinction which is drawn within Islam between the Qur'ān and Ḥadīth Qudsī. The word Ḥadīth means a record of the word or deed of the Prophet. In some of these, God is represented as saying something directly to the

Prophet, which he then reports as a statement made by God. Such statements made by God are never confused with the Qur'ān in the Islamic tradition, which *alone* represents the literal word of God. The other statements may be said to come from God but they are not statements of God in the sense the Qur'ān is.

This idea that according to Islam the Qur'ān is literally the word of God takes some time to sink in because the mind tends to baulk at it. But this is precisely the point — that is why the Qur'ān is considered a miracle, the miracle being that God's words became human words.

If this idea appears odd then the Hindu should consider the fact that the Hindu concept of revelation, according to its schools of Vedānta, is indeed equally odd — though in a different way. While Islam believes that God is literally the author of the Qur'ān, the Vedāntins believe that the Vedas have no author at all — human or divine. This is not the only view of revelation in Hinduism but it is the regnant one, specially so far as the school of Vedānta is concerned. J.A.B. van Buitenen makes the point well:

> If we are to form a proper understanding of the meaning and scope of "Revelation," we do well to forget at once the implications of the term in the Mediterranean religions, Judaism, Christianity, and Islam. Strictly speaking, "revelation" is a misnomer, since ultimately there is no revealer. The Sanskrit term for it is *śruti*, literally "the hearing," which means an erudition acquired by listening to the instruction of a teacher. This instruction itself had been transmitted to the teacher through an uninterrupted series of teachers that stretches to the beginning of creation.

Revelation, therefore, is by no means God's word — because, paradoxically, if it were to derive from a divine person, its credibility would be impugned. It is held to be authorless, for if a person, human or divine, had authored it, it would be vulnerable to the defects inherent in such a person. It is axiomatic that revelation is infallible, and this infallibility can be defended only if it is authorless.

Then from where does it come? The answer is stark and simple: it is given with the world. For some of the Mīmāṁsā (or orthodox, exegetical) thinkers who have addressed themselves to this problem, the world is beginningless and the assumption of a creator is both problematic and unnecessary. And even if a beginning of the world is assumed, as in later Hindu thought when it is held that the universe goes through a pulsating rhythm of origination, existence, and dissolution, it is also held that at the dawn of a new world the revelation reappears to the vision of the seers, who once more begin the transmission.[1]

II

A few words about the manner in which the Qur'ān assumed its present shape may be in order, now that the Islamic self-understanding of the Qur'ān has been presented.

It was noted earlier, while discussing the life of Prophet Muḥammad, that the first revelation was received by him

---

1. *See* Eliot Deutsch and Rohit Dalvi, *The Essential Vedānta: A New Source Book of Advaita Vedānta* (Bloomignton, Indiana: World Wisdom Inc., 2004), p. 3.

in 610. The first revelation was followed by many others, the Prophet receiving them until he died in 632. Thus the Qur'ān is a compilation of the revelations received by Prophet Muḥammad over this period of twenty-two years. During his lifetime people either memorized the revelations or wrote them down on parchments or bones and so on, and no concern was felt about their preservation in the face of the fact that the process of reception was still continuing. However, immediately after the death of prophet Muḥammad, many tribes who had entered into agreements with him began to claim that they had entered into an alliance with the Prophet, and not his successors, and reneged on them. This understanding was rejected by Abū Bakr and what have been called wars of apostasy (*ridda*) followed. In these battles many Muslims, who knew the Qur'ān by heart, perished. This is said to have aroused Abū Bakr's concern and the process of the compilation of the text was probably set in motion by him. In any case, the task was completed during the period of the third caliph, 'Uthmān (r. 644-56). In other words, in no more than twenty years after the Prophet's death an authorized version of the Qur'ān was produced.

> Since the time the Qur'ān has remained unchanged, except for adding vowel diacritics and minor adjustments in the ordering of certain verses. It was copied in manuscript until modern times, when the royal Egyptian edition produced in the 1930s became the most widely accepted printed text.[2]

2. Mahmoud M. Ayoub, op. cit., p. 372.

If we regard Islam as the youngest of the major religions of the world, and Hinduism the oldest, then the two traditions display a similar concern with the meticulous preservation of their revealed texts. It has been observed for instance regarding the Vedas that "the oral recensions of the texts have been maintained with meticulous precision for at least three millennia, and this has no parallel anywhere in the world."[3]

The Qur'ān consists of 114 *sūrah*s or chapters and is similar in size to the New Testament. "Tradition asserts that while the verses of each individual *sūrah* were arranged by the Prophet at Gabriel's instruction, the order of the *sūrah*s in relation to one another — roughly in decreasing order of length — was fixed by the committee that 'Uthmān appointed to compile an official recension of the Qur'ān."[4] Just as Hindu prayers might begin with *om*, each *sūrah* begins with the invocation *bism-illāhi ar-raḥmān ar-raḥīm* (in the name of God, the all-merciful, the compassionate) except for the ninth, which is treated as a continuation of the eighth.[5]

A distinct feature of the Qur'ān is the opening verse (*al-Fātiḥah*). It is often used as a general invocation, like the Lord's Prayer in Christianity, or like the famous invocation, much shorter by comparison, from the *Bṛhadāraṇyaka Upaniṣad* (I.3.28):

---

3. Edwin Byrant, *The Quest for the Origins of Vedic Culture: The Indo-Aryan Migration Debate* (New York: Oxford University Press, 2001), p. 251.
4. Mahmoud M. Ayoub, op. cit., p. 372.
5. Ibid.

From the unreal lead me to the real.
From darkness lead me to light.
From death lead me to immortality.[6]

The *al-Fātiḥah* reads as follows in translation:

THE OPENING

In the Name of God, the Merciful, the Compassionate

Praise belongs to God, the Lord of all Being,
the All-merciful, the All-compassionate,
the Master of the Day of Doom.

Thee only we serve; to Thee alone we pray for succour.

Guide us in the straight path,
the path of those whom Thou hast blessed,
not of those against whom Thou art wrathful,
nor of those who are astray.[7]

The Qur'ān was received either at Makkah or Madīnah and this is indicated with each chapter but because the *sūrahs* were arranged in descending order of length (but for the *al-Fātiḥah*) it is "impossible to determine with certainty the chronology of the recitation of the Qur'ān."[8]

---

6. S. Radhakrishnan, ed., *The Principal Upaniṣads* (Atlantic Heights, NJ: Humanities Press International, Inc., 1992 [1953]), p. 162.
7. Arthur J. Arberry, *The Koran Interpreted* (New York: The Macmillan Company, 1955), p. 29.
8. Mahmoud M. Ayoub, op. cit., p. 372.

Just as each hymn in the *R̥gVeda* has the metre, author and deity indicated for it, the circumstances in which the *sūrah* was received is provided by tradition for each chapter of the Qur'ān as constituting the "occasions of revelation" (*asbāb al-nuzūl*).[9]

On the intriguing question of how the revelations were received, Prophet Muḥammad described this process according to tradition as follows:

> Revelation sometimes comes like the sound of a bell; that is the most painful way. When it ceases I have remembered what was said. Sometimes it is an angel who talks to me like a human, and I remember what he says.[10]

The Hindu reader might wish to compare this with the description of revelation in Hinduism as *śruti*, or that which is heard.[11] Fazlur Rahman explains in relation to the Qur'ān:

---

9. Mahmoud M. Ayoub, p. 405.
10. Cited in Mary Pat Fisher, *Living Religions* (5th edn.) (Upper Saddle River, N.J.: Prentice-Hall, 2002), p. 362.
11. The following account of the manner of revelation of the Qur'ān by Fazlur Rahman, *Major Themes of the Qur'ān* (Minneapolis: Bibliotheca Islamica, 1980), p. 99 is also of interest:

    The question now is of the manner of Revelation.

    It does not belong to any human that God should speak to him (directly) except by Revelation (i.e. infusion of the Spirit) or from behind a veil (i.e. by a voice whose source is invisible) or that He should send a (spiritual) Messenger who reveals (to the Prophet) by God's permission what He wills — and He is exalted and Wise. And even so have We revealed unto you (i.e. infused in your →

That the Prophet actually mentally "heard" words is clear from 75:16-19: "Do not hasten your tongue with it [the Revelation] in order to anticipate it. It is our task to collect it and recite it. *So when We recite it, follow its recital,* and then it is also Our task to explain it" (see also 20:114). It is also clear that, in his anxiety to retain it or to "anticipate" it in a direction different from that of his Revealing Spirit, the Prophet moved his tongue of his own ordinary human volition, the intrusion of which was repudiated by God. This necessarily implies the total "otherness" of the agent of Revelation from the conscious personality of Muḥammad in the act of Revelation. But it is equally

---

→ *mind) the Spirit of Our Command — you did not know before what the Book is nor what Faith is, but We have made it a light whereby We guide whomsoever We will of our servants, and you, indeed, guide (people) to the straight path (42:51-52).*

What primarily concerns us here is the first part of this passage. What it tells us is that God never speaks directly to a human but He may infuse a Spirit in the Prophet's mind (as the next verse of the passage says of Muḥammad), (1) which makes him see the truth and utter it ("Say: This is my path — I call people [to God] on the basis of a clear perception" [12:108]; "He [Muḥammad] speaks not from his own desire — it is but a Revelation vouchsafed to him" [53:3]), or (2) which produces an actual mental sound, not a physical sound, and an idea-word, not a physically acoustic word; or (3) which takes on the form of a Messenger agent "giving" the Revelation to the Prophet. Whatever the agency of Revelation, however, the true revealing subject always remains God, for it is He Who always speaks in the first person and it is He Who speaks even in this passage, informing the Prophet that He has sent the "Spirit of Our Command to you."

> clear that the words heard were mental and not acoustic, since the spirit and the voice were internal to him.[12]

An interesting point of convergence between the Islamic and Hindu revelations is their 'sonorous' quality: the texts of the revelations are intended not just for reading but also for recitation. This performative dimension highlights their role in quickening the religious sensibility when they are *heard*, as distinguished from what is actually said. The Hindu may wish to consider the possibility of understanding the Qur'ān in terms of *śruti* both in respect to it being heard, as mentioned earlier, and in the sense of it being recited. Those Hindus who have experienced the spell cast by a Vedic or similar recitation may find echoes of it in the following account of Driss Chanbi, the émigré son who returns home for the funeral of the old father of the family from Paris:

> Then a man stood up . . . and began to chant. What he chanted was of no importance. It was not the words, nor the meaning, nor even the symbolism, which moved our hearts, the men, women and children who were there. We forgot why we were there the moment he began to chant. It was the incantation, and the end of our woes and miserable little problems, the aching and yet serene longing for that other life which is ours and to which we are all destined to return, the victors and the defeated, the fully developed and those who are still at the larva state, the faithful and the atheists, through God's great compassion. There was all of that in the voice of the man who stood chanting in the sun,

---

12. Fazlur Rahman, op. cit., pp. 99-100.

> and we were in his voice, I was in his voice despite the vast legacy of incredulity that I had received from the West. When he reached the end of a verse, he paused, and so it came about — an outburst of fervour. And while he chanted it was like a man in the wilderness chanting his faith. And the voice rose and swelled, changed in tone, became tragic, soared and then floated down on our heads like a seagull gliding gently and softly, little more than a whisper. And so — never again will I go in search of intellectuals, of written truths, synthetic truths, of collections of hybrid ideas which are nothing but ideas. Never again will I travel the world in search of a shadow of justice, fairness, progress, or schemes calculated to change mankind. I was weary and I was returning to my clan. The man who was not even aware of his voice or of his faith was alive and held the secret of life — a man who could not even have been a dustman in this world of founts of knowledge and of civilization. Peace and everlasting truth were in him and in his voice, while all was crumbling around him and on the continents.[13]

The effect of the recitation produced on the young man may help us appreciate the concept of the inimitability of the Qur'ān which Fazlur Rahman elaborates as follows:

> There is a vast literature in Islam known as *i'jāz al-Qur'ān* setting out the doctrine of the "inimitability of the Qur'ān." This doctrine takes it rise from the Qur'ān itself, for the Qur'ān proffers itself as the unique

---

13. Driss Chanbi, cited in T. Patrick Burke, *The Major Religions: An Introduction with Texts* (Malden, MA: Blackwell Publishing, 2004), pp. 265-66.

miracle of Muḥammad. No other revealed Book is described in the Qur'ān as a miracle in this way except the Qur'ān itself; it follows that not all embodiments of Revelations are miracles, even though the event of Revelation itself is a kind of miracle. The Qur'ān emphatically challenges its opponents to "bring forth one *sura* like those of the Qur'ān" (2:23) and "to call upon anyone except God" to achieve this (10:38; cf. 11:13, which is probably earlier). There is a consensus among those who know Arabic well, and who appreciate the genius of the language, that in the beauty of its language and the style and power of its expression the Qur'ān is a superb document. The linguistic nuances simply defy translation. Although all inspired language is untranslatable, this is even more the case with the Qur'ān.[14]

14. Fazlur Rahman, op. cit., pp. 104-05.

4

The Pillars of Islam

I

THE use of the expression — "Pillars of Islam" — might at first sight appear to be a matter of English phrasing of the basic principles of Islam. It is therefore salutary to be reminded that the expression is itself a part of the Islamic tradition, which uses the word *arkān* or pillars to refer to the five foundational dimensions of the faith. "A well-attested prophetic tradition characterizes Islam as built upon five 'pillars.'"[1] This clarity in the formulation of its doctrines and practices is also worth noting, in the face of the complexity if not confusion which accompanies any attempt to formulate the basic principles and practices of Hinduism.[2] In Hinduism such clarity is oftener found at the level of sect (or *sampradāya*) rather than religion. These five pillars are the following:

(1) Shahādah (bearing witness)

(2) Ṣalāt (prayer)

(3) Ẓakāt (almsgiving)

---

1. Mahmoud M. Ayoub, op. cit., p. 376.

2. For a recent effort by the Supreme Court to do so see Mary Pat Fischer, *Living Religions* (5th edn.) (Upper Saddle River, N.J.: Prentice-Hall, 2002), pp. 125-26.

(4) Ṣawm (fasting during Ramaḍān)

(5) Ḥajj (pilgrimage to Makkah)

SHAHĀDAH

The *shahādah* constitutes the profession of faith in Islam and consists of the following statement: *lā ilāha illa allāhu muḥammad ur-rasūl ullāh*: There is no god but God and Muḥammad is His messenger.[3] Both segments of the *shahādah* are found in the Qur'ān, although they do not occur together therein. Anyone who repeats this statement with the *intention* of embracing Islam once in his life, before two Muslim witnesses, is thereafter accepted as a Muslim and may not be excluded from any gathering of Muslims. "There is no other ceremony required for one to become a Muslim."[4] Thereafter, if one does not follow the precepts of Islam one could be labelled a bad Muslim but one may not be called a non-Muslim. In making the statement of faith, *niyah* or intention, is all-important, for otherwise the statement is made by one who is teaching a class on Islam many a time but it acquires the power of a faith statement only through intention. The question might be asked — when anyone states his or her intention, how do we know that it is sincere? The answer is that we don't — that truth is known only to God and that henceforth is a matter between him or her and God. Once a person has borne witness in the manner described, a person is to be accepted as a Muslim.

The two components of the *shahādah* need to be examined closely. One should note that Arabic does not

3. For the Arabic text in Roman script, see H.A.R. Gibb, op. cit., p. 183.

4. Mahmoud M. Ayoub, op. cit., p. 376.

employ capital letters, although in the English rendering the word God has been capitalized in the second occurrence. But it places the emphasis where it belongs, for the statement is a celebration of absolute monotheism. God alone exists and placing any partners beside him is *shirk*, the worst form of heresy in Islam. Allah was one of the many gods worshipped by the Arabs. It was now raised to the status of the sole God. Allah is the only word for God in general in Arabic so that Arab Christians also use it as a word for God.

Attention has been drawn by Mahmoud M. Ayoub to a point of great historical significance in relation to this first half of the *shahādah*, as follows:

> It seems that initially only the first declaration of the *shahādah* was required of non-Muslims to be admitted into the Muslim *ummah*, or at least to be granted the legal status of a protected people: Jews, Christians, and other scriptural communities or "People of the Book." This conclusion is supported by another widely accepted tradition, in which the Prophet says:
>
> I have been commanded to wage war against people until they say "There is no god except God." When they say this, they protect from me their lives and their possessions, except what is required of them (as the *ẓakāt* alms), and their final reckoning is with God.[5]

Islamic mystics or *ṣūfīs* have sometimes offered a mystical interpretation of the first half of the *shahādah* as follows: that one has to pass through a period of "doubt" about the reality of God before one arrives at the firm conviction of the reality of God.

5. Mahmoud M. Ayoub, op. cit., p. 376.

Implicit in the claim that there is only one God is the rejection not only of polytheism but also of the form in which such polytheism is usually expressed, namely, idolatry. The shrine of Ka'bah was cleared of all images after the return of the Prophet to Makkah. According to one tradition it contained an image for each day of the year. One can now see how Muslims can quickly and perhaps rashly conclude that Hindus are polytheists because of the extravagant presence of images within Hinduism. It is hard for a person, who associates a multiplicity of images with polytheism, to appreciate the idea that Hinduism is really monotheistic. The fact that these many images directly or indirectly point to only one God may be initially hard to comprehend.

One accepts Muḥammad as a messenger of God by bearing witness to the second half of the *shahādah*. Two points need to be particularly noted in this regard. Two Arabic words are used to designate the person we have been referring to as a prophet — *rasūl* and *nabī*. In many contexts the distinction is not significant but when it is drawn the distinction rests on the ground that a *rasūl* is a messenger of God and therefore brings a message from God, while a *nabī* (literally a prophet) warns people about the danger of ignoring such messages and guides them according to it. One way of bringing out the distinction between the two would be to say that a *rasūl* brings the Law, while a *nabī* brings the people to the Law. But the distinction should not be overdone because all messengers are prophets, although all prophets are not messengers. For instance, Muḥammad is referred to as a messenger in the *shahādah* but in the statement in the Qur'ān according to which the line of prophecy is closed according to Muslims,

Muḥammad is called the "seal of the prophets" (Qur'ān 25:30).

It is important to recognize the sub-text of the statement that Muḥammad is the messenger of God, namely, that he is the *last messenger*. The Arab account regarding Ishmael was referred to earlier. "Following Ishmael's line in Arabia, we come to the latter half of the sixth century CE to Muhammad, the prophet through whom Islam reached its definitive form, Muslims believe. There had been authentic prophets of God before him, but he was their culmination; hence he is called 'the seal of the Prophets.' No valid prophets will follow him."[6] The word valid is important, for some have claimed the status of being a prophet after Muḥammad, but the claim has been rejected by Muslims. The founder of the Ahmadiyyah movement claimed that status and that is why although the Ahmadiyyahs consider themselves Muslim, the Muslims do not regard them as such.

It should be remembered that the claim — that Muḥammad is the final prophet — has more to do with his function than status, although one could detect the idea of a continuous progressive revelation underlying it, in the sense that the Qur'ān is a pure revelation, while the preceding ones have become corrupted. There are two Hindu concepts analogous to the idea that a later prophet may have greater authority and a later text of revelation may in some sense supersede earlier ones. There is "a maxim current among grammarians — *yathottaram munīnām prāmāṇyam*. That is to say: 'The later the sage, the greater

6. Huston Smith, *The World's Religions*, p. 223.

his authority.'"[7] Similarly, the school of Śuddhādvaita Vedānta, associated with the name of Vallabha (1473–1531), accepts "Four canonical texts arranged in the following order: (i) The Veda (including the Upaniṣads), (ii) The *Gītā*, (iii) The *Vedānta-sūtra,* and (iv) The *Bhāgavata.* Vallabha's view is that these texts are complementary to one another, that where doubts arise, each preceding text should be interpreted in the light of the next."[8] These elements in the Hindu tradition, it is easy to see, bear a family resemblance to the Islamic ideas as related to the Prophet and the Qur'ān discussed above, specially the idea that the Qur'ān fulfils and confirms the previous revelations received by the Jews and the Christians.

This belief has important implications for the Muslim attitude towards the Jews and Christians. Muslims see themselves standing squarely in the tradition of prophecy[9] shared by all of them, which is now concluded in prophet Muḥammad. This view, regarding the indivisibility of prophecy, makes it a matter of genuine puzzlement for Muslims that the Jews and the Christians don't accept the Islamic dispensation. This point is made with great clarity by Patrick Burke in the following passage:

> Although non-Muslims view Islam as the youngest of the major religions, Islam does not regard itself in the same way. It sees itself as identical with the first

---

7. M. Hiriyanna, *Popular Essays in Indian Philosophy* (Mysore: Kavyalaya Publishers, 1952), p. 75.

8. T.M.P. Mahadevan, *Outlines of Hinduism,* (Bombay: Chetana Limited, 1971), p. 162.

9. See Fazlur Rahman, op. cit., p. 164.

> revelation God gave to mankind. The Koran mentions some 25 individuals to whom God gave the essentials of the Koranic message in earlier times. These are the prophets. A prophet in this sense is not necessarily a person who predicts the future, but one who speaks on behalf of God. They include Adam, Noah, Abraham (Ibrahim), Joseph (Yusuf), Moses (Musa), Aaron (Harun), David (Dawud), John the Baptist (Yahya), and Jesus (Isa). All of these were Muslims.
>
> To each one God entrusted a scripture, containing essentially the same message as the Koran: of submission to God; to Moses, for example, he gave the Torah; to David the Psalms; to Jesus the Gospel. But in each case the scriptures were corrupted or misinterpreted. As a result these texts have no authority for Muslims. It was to correct these distortions that God sent Mohammed, revealing to him again the true Koran. It alone is now the pure scripture, possessing the original form given it by God, and so it supersedes all the earlier ones.
>
> Islam, then, is simply the true form of what Judaism and Christianity ought to be and would be if they had remained faithful to their original inspiration.[10]

Belief in the prophethood of Muḥammad entails several allied beliefs such as belief in God, his messengers, angels, revealed books, heaven and hell, and the Last Day.

ṢALĀT (PRAYER)

The second pillar of Islam consists of the five obligatory

10. Patrick Burke, *The Major Religions: An Introduction with Texts* (Malden, MA: Blackwell Publishing, 2004), p. 271.

prayers called *ṣalāt*, which are to be distinguished from prayers one might offer of one's accord and which are called *du'ā*. "*Ṣalāt* must be performed five times in a day and night: at dawn, noon, mid-afternoon, sunset, and after dark. Among the rituals of Islam, the *ṣalāt* prayers were the first to be instituted."[11] They are to be preceded by ritual cleaning for which water or even sand could be used.

These prayers follow a standard format which differs slightly from prayer to prayer. The actual prayer consists of a combination of utterances with accompanying movements of the body, which include placing one's hands on the side of the head, kneeling and genuflection. These movements are called *rak'ah*s. The *al-Fātiḥah,* or the opening verse of the Qur'ān, is frequently repeated in the course of these prayers.

There is no fixed day like Sunday for communal worship in Islam. One comes closest to it in the prayers offered on Friday at noon, known as the Jum'ah prayers. The *ṣalāt* can be performed almost anywhere, "even so, Muslims are expected to pray in mosques when they can, and the Friday noon prayer is emphasized in this respect. Visitors to Muslim lands testify that one of the impressive religious sights in the world comes to view, when, in a dimly lighted mosque, hundreds of Muslims stand shoulder to shoulder, then repeatedly kneel and prostrate themselves toward Mecca."[12]

ẒAKĀT

The third pillar of Islam consists of alms-giving. In the early

11. Mahmoud M. Ayoub, op. cit., p. 378.

12. Huston Smith, op. cit., p. 245.

centuries of its history it was collected by the state but has since been left to individual initiative. It is disbursed annually and consists of a 2.5 per cent of the value of all accumulated wealth, or broadly assets. One again this obligatory alms-giving should be distinguished from voluntary alms-giving called *ṣadaqah*. *Ẓakāt* should be given to the poor "and to whom among the poor should this money be given? This too is prescribed: to those in immediate need; to slaves in the process of buying their freedom; to debtors unable to meet their obligations; to strangers and wayfarers; and to those who collect and distribute alms."[13]

The spiritual and moral significance of *ẓakāt* and *ṣadaqah* are worth noting. The word *ẓakāt* literally comes from a verb which means to purify. In a sense then one legitimizes the owning of one's private property through sharing a part of it with the community. The wealth spent in *ṣadaqah* is similarly considered a loan to God, which will be repaid handsomely on the day of judgement.

ṢAWM (FASTING)

Fasting during the month of Ramaḍān was instituted after the battle of Badr, which was fought and won in 624 in the month of Ramaḍān. This month is considered particularly auspicious in Islam because it was also the month in which the first revelation was received by the Prophet. Tradition even goes further and maintains that "not only the Qur'ān but other scriptures — the Torah, the Psalms (*Ẓabūr*), and the Gospel (*injīl*) — were also revealed in Ramaḍān."[14]

---

13. Huston Smith, op. cit., pp. 246-47.

14. Mahmoud M. Ayoub, op. cit., p. 382.

Ramaḍān can fall at any time of the year because the Islamic calendar is based on the moon and the lunar year consists of 354 days, as against the solar year of 365 days. During the month of Ramaḍān one is forbidden to eat or drink from dawn to dusk — even swallowing one's saliva amounts to breaking it, as a finer point of law. In order to sustain themselves during this period, people eat after sunset and before daybreak. The month-long fast concludes with the sighting of the moon and is celebrated with the festival called *'Īd al-Fiṭr* which lasts for three days, marked by feasting and the distribution of alms. Huston Smith's remarks on the observance of this fast are worth citing:

> Why, then, does the Koran require it? For one thing, fasting makes one think as every Jew who has observed the fast of Yom Kippur will attest. For another thing, fasting teaches self-discipline; one who can endure its demands will have less difficulty controlling the demands of appetites at other times. Fasting underscores the creature's dependence on God. Human beings, it is said, are as frail as rose petals; nevertheless, they assume airs and pretensions. Fasting calls one back to one's frailty and dependence. Finally, fasting sensitizes compassion. Only those who have been hungry can know what hunger means. People who have fasted for twenty-nine days within the year will be apt to listen more carefully when next approached by someone who is hungry.[15]

ḤAJJ (PILGRIMAGE)

Islam requires the every able-bodied Muslim, who can afford it, undertake a pilgrimage to Ka'bah at least once in his

15. Huston Smith, op. cit., p. 247.

lifetime. Although it may be undertaken at any time, it is specially recommended during the twelfth month of the Islamic calendar known as *Dhū al-Ḥijjah*. All the pilgrims don a pair of white linen sheets prior to the pilgrimage which are "symbolic of the shrouds in which people are wrapped for burial."[16] The pilgrims are now in a special state of sanctity called *iḥrām*.

The pilgrimage has two phases — the lesser one (*'umrah*) and pilgrimage proper. The lesser pilgrimage involves the circumambulation of the Ka'bah. Specially suggestive during this period is the running between the two hills of al-Ṣafā and al-Marwā. "In the traditional narrative Hagar, Abraham's handmaid and mother of his son Ishmael, runs between these two hills in search of water for her dying child. After the seventh run, water gushes out by the child's feet, which Hagar contains with hands. The place, according to Islamic tradition, is the ancient well of *zamzam*, meaning the 'contained water.' The water of *zamzam* is regarded by Muslims as holy water, and pilgrims often bring back containers of it as blessed gifts for family and friends."[17]

The high point of the main pilgrimage consists of the moment when, after spending the night at Minā one stands on the plain of 'Arafāt, and spends time in devotion from noon to sunset. "This rite links the present moment to the sacred time, to the time when Adam and Eve stand on that plain after their expulsion from paradise. It recalls the time when Abraham and his son Ishmael performed the rite. According to Muslim tradition they performed the first *ḥajj*

16. Mahmoud M. Ayoub, op. cit., p. 383.

17. Ibid., p. 384.

pilgrimage."[18] It is on this plain that prophet Muḥammad made his famous farewell oration, in which he declared that each Muslim is a brother to the other.

The circumambulation of the Ka'bah marks the end of *ḥajj*, followed by the offering of sacrifices.[19]

II

These then are the five Pillars of Islam and the reader would have noticed that but for the first they focus on orthopraxy.

---

18. Mahmoud M. Ayoub, op. cit., p. 384.

19. The mystical tradition within Islam offers its own interpretation of the pilgrimage as follows (Reynold A. Nicholson, *The Mystics of Islam* [London: Penguin Books, 1989 (1914)], p. 91:

    A man who had just returned from the pilgrimage came to Junayd. Junayd said: "From the hour when you first journeyed from your home have you also been journeying away from all sins?" He said "No." "Then," said Junayd, "you have made no journey. At every stage where you halted for the night did you traverse a station on the way to God?" "No," he replied. "Then," said Junayd, "you have not trodden the road, stage by stage. When you put on the pilgrim's garb at the proper place, did you discard the qualities of human nature as you cast off your clothes?" "No." "Then you have not put on the pilgrim's garb. When you stood at 'Arafāt, did you stand one moment in contemplation of God?" "No." "Then you have not stood at 'Arafāt. When you went to Muzdalifa and achieved your desire, did you renounce all sensual desires?" "No." "Then you have not gone to Muzdalifa. When you circumambulated the Ka'bah, did you behold the immaterial beauty of God in the abode of purification?" "No." "Then

→

"As both Muslim and non-Muslim scholars have observed, Islam is more concerned with orthopraxy than orthodoxy."[20] However, while Islam may be more concerned with orthopraxy than orthodoxy, a claim which has also been made about Hinduism, this does not mean that it does not possess a set of beliefs. This was hinted at towards the end of the discussion of the first pillar of Islam and thread may now be carried forward.

God

One begins of course with belief in one God, as celebrated in the *shahādah*. The knowledge of this one God was communicated by this one God through an angel to the Prophet.

Islam thus implies belief in an angelic order of beings, or the existence of spiritual beings apart from human beings. In this respect Gabriel is particularly important. Michael is also mentioned in the Qur'ān.[21] However, besides the

---

→ you have not circumambulated the Ka'bah. When you ran between Saf'ā and Marwa, did you attain to purity (*safā*) and virtue (*muruwwat*)?" "No." "Then you have not run. When you came to Minā, did all your wishes (*munā*) cease?" "No." "Then you have not yet visited Minā. When you reached the slaughter-place and offered sacrifice, did you sacrifice the objects of worldly desire?" "No." "Then you have not sacrificed. When you threw the pebbles, did you throw away whatever sensual thoughts were accompanying you?" "No." "Then you have not yet thrown the pebbles, and you have not yet performed the pilgrimage."

20. Mahmoud M. Ayoub, op. cit., p. 376.
21. Patrick Burke, op. cit., p. 271.

angels, there is another kind of being called the *jinn* (plural; the singular is *jinni*, the origin of the "genie" in the story of Alādīn's lamp). The *jinn* is created by God out of fire and, unlike the angels, they eventually die. They are both sexes and can be good or evil. *Iblis*, or Satan, is a *jinni*."[22] The Prophet is depicted as preaching to the *jinn* after he was turned away from Ṭaif.

Prophets

God's messages to human beings are mediated through the categories of people described as *nabī*, literally meaning a "giver of news," and it is worth noting that it "does not mean in the Qur'ān (as it mostly did in the Bible) 'one who gives news about the future,' but 'one who gives news from God.'"[23] *Rasūl* means messenger — that is messenger of God to mankind "although in the Qur'ān . . . this term is also sometimes applied to the angel of revelation, one who is sent by God to the prophet."[24] It is also important to note, in relation to the discussion of revelation which is to follow, that "traditionally, Muslim Qur'ān commentators have made a distinction, saying the *nabī* means a divine envoy without a law (*sharī'a*) and, presumably, without a revealed book, while *rasūl* means one with a law and a revealed book."[25] Fazlur Rahman clarifies the situation in this regard in relation to the Qur'ān as follows:

---

22. Patrick Burke, op. cit., p. 271.
23. Fazlur Rahman, op. cit., p. 82.
24. Ibid.
25. Ibid.

> Although such sharp distinctions are somewhat doubtful, since the Qur'ān describes some religious personages both as *nabī* and as *rasūl* (e.g. 7:158; 19:51, 54), there is no doubt that some distinction is intended, for example, in a verse like "And We did not send before you any *rasūl* or *nabī*" (22:52). It also appears that the frequency of use of *nabī* increases from the later Meccan period through the Madinan period. On the whole *rasūl* does signify something weightier than *nabī*, for a *nabī* can be auxiliary to a *rasūl* as Aaron was to Moses (19:51, 53), although *rasūl*s (or, strictly speaking *mursala*, "the one sent") can be jointly commissioned (36:13, 16). Although prophecy is indivisible (2:136), not all prophets are equal, for "We have made some Messengers more excellent than others" (2:253; also see 17:55) and Muḥammad is exhorted to "be patient [under trial] as the Messengers with determination and steadfastness were patient" (46:35).[26]

The important point to keep in mind is that, according to the Qur'ān, prophets have been sent to all the people. Two points need to be clearly understood here: that the Qur'ān mentions twenty-six prophets by name, which include Abraham, Moses, Solomon, Elijah, Jonah, John the Baptist and Jesus among them,[27] and that apart from these biblical figures it also mentions three Arabian prophets: Shu'ayb, Hūd and Ṣāliḥ, which means that Arabia possessed an independent tradition of prophecy.

---

26. Fazlur Rahman, op. cit., p. 82.

27. Mahmoud M. Ayoub, op. cit., p. 363.

> The chronology of the major prophets as it can be ascertained from suras 7 and 11 — which give their accounts systematically, especially surah 11, which has a developed and patterned style — is: Noah, Hūd, Ṣāliḥ, Abraham (whose contemporary is Lot), Shu'aib (who is placed not much after Lot and Abraham 11:89), Moses and Jesus. Except for Noah, the two Arabian prophets are the more ancient than the entire biblical tradition.[28]

Revelations

It is a belief in Islam that all the peoples of the world have been vouchsafed a messenger: "Verily to every people there is a messenger" (X.48) and therefore a revelation. The message however in many cases has not been preserved in its purity and is thought to have been corrupted.

Resurrection and the Last Judgement

The Qur'ān indicates that the Arabs, prior to the coming of Muḥammad, did not believe in an afterlife. The Qur'ān however introduced the doctrine of resurrection and contains vivid descriptions of the Day of Judgement.

III

These then are the five pillars of Islam. The fact that they refer largely to external observances or beliefs should not be taken to mean that the subtler dimensions of religion are overlooked in Islam. The following saying of the Prophet, transmitted by 'Umar, provides a healthy corrective to this view.

---

28. Fazlur Rahman, op. cit., p. 83.

One day when we were sitting with the Messenger of God there came unto us a man whose clothes were of exceeding whiteness and whose hair was of exceeding blackness, nor were there any signs of travel upon him, although none of us knew him. He sat down knee unto knee opposite the Prophet, upon whose thighs he placed the palms of his hands saying: "O Muḥammad, tell me what is the surrender (*islām*)." The Messenger of God answered him saying: "The surrender is to testify that there is no god but God and that Muḥammad is God's Messenger, to perform the prayer, bestow the alms, fast Ramaḍān and make, if thou canst, the pilgrimage to the Holy House." He said: "Thou hast spoken truly," and we were amazed that having questioned him he should corroborate him. Then he said: "Tell me what is faith (*īmān*)." He answered: "To believe in God and His Angels and His Books and His Messengers and the Last Day, and to believe that no good or evil cometh but by His Providence." "Thou hast spoken truly," he said, and then: "Tell me what is excellence (*iḥsān*)." He answered: "To worship God as if thou sawest Him, for if thou seest Him not, yet seeth He thee." "Thou hast spoken truly," he said, and then: "Tell me of the Hour." He answered: "The questioned thereof knoweth no better than the questioner." He said: "Then tell me of its signs." He answered: "That the slave-girl shall give birth to her mistress; and that those who were but barefoot naked needy herdsmen shall build buildings ever higher and higher." Then the stranger went away, and I stayed a while after he had gone; and the Prophet said to me: "O 'Umar, knowest thou the questioner, who he was?" I said: "God and His Messenger know best." He said: "It was Gabriel. He came unto you to teach you your religion."[29]

29. Cited in Seyyed Hossein Nasr, "Islam", in Arvind Sharma, ed., op. cit., p. 471.

5

Islamic Law

THE word used by Muslims for what is commonly referred to as Islamic law outside the Muslim world is *sharī'a*. The word literally means the way to the watering place but its connotation is more important than its denotation. It means the Way one should lead one's life so that it conforms to God's will. While skeptics and philosophers are concerned with the question whether God exists or not (and some Muslim skeptics and philosophers may have shared this predisposition) the starting point assumed by Islam is rather different. It begins by assuming the existence of God, so for it the key question is: What does God want us to do?

In this sense the use of the word law for *sharī'a* offers a somewhat restricted perspective on it. *Sharī'a* deals with the question of leading a life informed with proper norms — with leading the normative life. The process was set in motion when the Muslim community in Medina took shape and continued with the rapid expansion of Islam after the death of the Prophet. After the Prophet, the *sharī'a* crystallized as the Islamic way of life and has continued to guide Muslims since.

The basic issue is to determine how one should act in a particular situation. The *sharī'a* developed a procedure for how to proceed when one wanted to know what is the right way to proceed. This principle is embodied in the doctrine of *uṣūl* or the principles.

The principle underlying the principles works as follows. The first source to consult on a matter of law or behaviour one seeks guidance on was the Qur'ān, for it lays down the general ethical framework out of which one operates. One should not infer from the fact of the Qur'ān being the first source of the *sharī'a* that the Qur'ān is legalistic. It has been pointed out that the "Qur'ān does not promulgate absolute laws, even where it strictly demands the severe punishment of the thief, adulterer, or murderer. It is more concerned with moral issues in actual life situations. Among its over 6000 verses, no more than 200 are explicitly legislative." But the Qur'ān is the word of God and thus constitutes the highest possible authority on any matter.

Should the matter not be resolved by reference to the Qur'ān as such, one then turned to the next source: the *sunnah*, or the practice of prophet Muḥammad. Mahmoud M. Ayoub explains the role of *sunnah* as a source of the *sharī'a* as follows:

> The Prophet reportedly declared, "I was given the Qur'ān and its equivalent (i.e. the *sunnah*) along with it." Hence, Muslims believe the Prophet's actions and sayings are divinely inspired. The Qur'ān asserts that God has sent his Messenger with "the Book and wisdom" (see Qur'ān 62:2). Al-Shāfi'ī, the architect of Islamic jurisprudence and founder of one of the four Sunnī legal schools, argued that "the Book" is the Qur'ān and "the wisdom" is the *sunnah*. His view has been generally accepted by Muslims.

The Prophet's *sunnah* includes his actions and his tacit consent. His acts are reported in anecdotes of situations or events to which he reacted or in which he participated. In situations where the Prophet neither approved nor objected, his silence is taken to signify approval. Thus the *sunnah* of consent became a normative source in the development of Islamic law.

Beside the *sunnah* of action and the *sunnah* of consent, there is the *sunnah* of speech. Accounts that report the Prophet's sayings, termed *ḥadīth*, must go back to an eyewitness to the event. The *ḥadīth* literature is often called "tradition" in English, in a quite specific sense. Islamic "tradition" (or "Prophetic tradition") is the body of sayings traced to the prophet Muḥammad through chains of oral transmission. *Ḥadīth* is the most important of the three elements of *sunnah*, since it most directly expresses the Prophet's opinions or judgements regarding the community's practice.[1]

The question naturally arises: How do we know what the Prophet did, said or accepted? The answer is provided by six thick volumes of what are called *ḥadīth* collections, the two best known among them being those compiled by Muḥammad B. Ismā'īl al-Bukhārī (810-70) and Muslim B. al-Ḥajjāj al-Nīsābūrī (*c.* 817-75). These "two collections, entitled simply *Ṣaḥīḥ al-Bukhārī* and *Ṣaḥīḥ Muslim*, soon achieved canonical status, second in authority to the *Qur'ān*. Although the *Ṣaḥīḥ* of Muslim is better organized and methodologically superior to that of al-Bukhārī, the latter has achieved first place among all *ḥadīth* collections."[2]

1. Mahmoud M. Ayoub, op. cit., pp. 371-72.

2. Ibid., p. 408.

Between them the two collections contain about 3000 *ḥadīths*. The authority of a *ḥadīth* rests on its authenticity, which rests on the reliability of the chain of transmission called *isnād*, and the aim of *ḥadīth* studies is basically to establish its authenticity. If the question for instance is: Should I pray in ordinary or fancy clothes, then the answer is provided by a *ḥadīth* which records that the Prophet was once given a silken garment as a gift but after performing his prayers he said it is not proper to pray in this manner.

If a clear indication was not forthcoming either from the Qur'ān or the *sunnah*, then one resorted to *qiyās* or analogical reasoning. The classical example of such reasoning is provided by the punishment for consuming liquor prescribed in *sharī'a*. The Qur'ān advises against drinking but does not prescribe any punishment for doing so. However it does prescribe a certain number of lashes for loose talk. Since drinking liquor makes one talk loosely, the same number of lashes were prescribed as punishment for drinking liquor.

Finally, if none of these avenues provide a satisfactory answer one turns to the *ijmā'* or the consensus of the community. This principle is based on a famous statement of the Prophet in the course of the farewell speech that "my followers will never agree in an error."

Should it turn out to be the case that resort to any of these four principles (1) Qur'ān; (2) *sunnah*; (3) *qiyās* and (4) *ijmā'* is unavailing, then one engaged in the creative process of struggling to determine how God's law may be applied to the present situation. This process is called *ijtihād* and we already got a hint of this in the process of *qiyās*.

This determination of the right course of conduct for a Muslim to follow was obviously not something which every Muslim did on his own; rather, as in modern society, one turned to the experts for guidance. Such an expert, a learned person, is called an *ālim* in Arabic, so that the judgement of such scholars (in the plural) called the *'ulamā'* provided the required guidance to the community.

These religious scholars played a major role in shaping the edifice of Islamic law in the first three centuries, after which it was firmly in place. By now five schools of *sharī'a* had evolved. which differed on points of detail while broadly adopting a similar approach. These schools, named after their main founding figures, are known as the (1) Ḥanbalī; (2) Ḥanafī; (3) Shāfi'ī and (4) Mālikī schools of Sunnī Islam, while the fifth school, that of (5) Ja'farī, pertained to Shī'ī Islam. They gained following in different parts of the world. The Ḥanabalī school is represented in Saudi Arabia, for instance, the Ḥanafī in South Asia, the Shāfi'ī in Indonesia, the Mālikī in North Africa and the Jāfarī in Iran. These represent the primary geographical areas to which the schools belong and should not leave one with the impression that other schools are totally unrepresented there.

The principles of Islamic law or *uṣūl* show a remarkable convergence with principles of Hindu jurisprudence. The word *dharma* denotes right conduct in Hinduism. Now if we raise the question: How do we find out what the *dharma* is in a particular situation? then the *Manusmṛti* identifies four such sources of *dharma* (*dharma-mūla*): (1) *śruti*, (2) *smṛti*, (3) *ācāra*, and (4) *ātma-tuṣṭi*. *Śruti* stands for Revelation, *smṛti* for Tradition, *ācāra* for the norms of conduct established by noble people and *ātma-tuṣṭi* for what we would now call conscience. It is hard to miss the broad similarity of pattern in determining the right course of action in Islam and Hinduism. The parallel between Qur'ān and *śruti* is obvious. *Ḥadīth*, from a Hindu point of view, represents the combination of *smṛti* and *ācāra* in relation to the Prophet. Even here the existence of different *smṛtis* may be compared to the existence of various schools in Islam. *Ijmā'* in Islam may be interpreted as the "conscience of the community." Hence the same basic principles seem to be at work, although the level at which they work, individual or collective, seems to differ.

Some provisions in the Hindu *smṛtis* also are reminiscent of some provisions of the *sharī'a*. One is familiar with the requirement that food consumed by a Muslim should be *ḥalāl*. A verse in the *Manusmṛti* (V. 36) reads: "A brāhmaṇa must never eat animals that have not been consecrated with ritual formulas. Abiding by the eternal rule, however, he must eat those that have been consecrated with ritual formulas."[3] Similarly, readers may be familiar with the provision in the *sharī'a*, involving amputation of limbs for theft. Two verses in the *Manusmṛti* (IX. 276-77) run as follows: "When robbers cut through walls and commit theft at night, the king should cut off their hands and impale them on sharp stakes. After the first offence, he should have two fingers of a pick pocket cut off; after the second, the hands and feet; and after the third, he ought to be executed."[4]

---

3. Patrick Olivelle, *The Law Code of Manu*, New York: Oxford University Press, 2004, p. 87.

4. Ibid., p. 175.

6

The History of Islam

It is a remarkable fact that although "within less than a century after the Prophet's death, the Muslims came to administer the largest dominion until that time the world had ever known,"[1] yet "Muḥammad left no political system for a world empire, nor any clear designation of a leader to succeed him nor any specific guidelines for choosing one."[2] We noted earlier how this vacuum created after his death was filled by Abū Bakr (632-34), but it did create a vortex out of which the community emerged partially divided. The background for what ensued is provided by the fact that when the Prophet migrated from Makkah to Medina, some of his followers migrated with him and were called *muhājir*s or Migrants, some of whom belonged to his tribe, which was Quraysh, and his clan, which was Hashim. Then there were the people of Medina who had helped the Prophet to migrate and they were called *anṣār* or Helpers. When the prophet died at Medina, the Helpers were all set to elect a leader when some of the close associates of the Prophet such as Abū Bakr and 'Umar rushed to the scene and we saw earlier how the commotion which followed ended with

---

1. Mahmoud M. Ayoub, op. cit., p. 386.
2. Ibid.

the acceptance of Abū Bakr as the successor or *khalīfah* of the Prophet. But his election accentuated the division between the *muhājirs* and the *anṣārs* on the one hand, and the Hashimites and other clans of the Quraysh tribe on the another. It remained below the surface so long as Abū Bakr was engaged in subduing the tribes who refused to pay *ẓakāt* (which the reader will recall, was collected at this time by the state) because they claimed their pact had been rendered inoperative by the death of the Prophet.

Abū Bakr was successful in his campaigns but at his death the question of succession was put in abeyance by the fact that he appointed 'Umar to succeed him. 'Umar (634-44) was originally called the "successor to the successor of the prophet" but perhaps as a result of the rapid conquest of Syria, Palestine, Jordan, Iraq and Iran during his reign he more fittingly adopted the title of the "Commander of the Faithful." He was assassinated by a Persian slave while leading the morning prayers in the Prophet's mosque at Medina,[3] which was still the capital of the realm. But before dying he had put together a committee of six to choose a successor. The two main candidates to emerge were 'Alī — the Prophet's son-in-law who of course belonged to the Prophet's clan and 'Uthmān who belonged to the Ummayyad clan. 'Uthmān was chosen over 'Alī but not without considerable conflict. 'Uthmān (644-56) however was accused of nepotism when he failed to investigate the charges of corruption against a relative who was the governor of Egypt. 'Uthmān prevaricated and the situation went out of control, when his house was

---

3. Mahmoud M. Ayoub, op. cit., p. 389.

besieged by an angry mob for forty days at the end of which he was killed. A relative of 'Uthmān, Mu'āwiyah, who was the governor of Damascus, demanded revenge, while displaying the blood-stained shirt of 'Uthmān. At this point 'Alī (656-61) was declared as the fourth Caliph in Medina but Mu'āwiyah accused him of inaction in punishing the murderers, virtually requiring this as a condition of 'Ali's legitimacy. This led to a military confrontation between the two at Siffīn in 657. "As the protracted battle turned in 'Alī's favour, Mu'āwiyah's men lifted up copies of the *Qur'ān* on the tips of the spears and called for God to judge among the people. Fighting ceased and two arbiters were chosen. Their negotiations in turn were inconclusive, and matters remained unresolved."[4] Some of 'Alī's followers, however, accused him of unbelief in accepting human arbitration in place of God's judgement and turned against him, being known as Khārijīs or dissenters on that account. They also dissented from the view gaining ground that the Caliph must come from the Prophet's tribe, the Quraysh, and espoused other radical ideas which now brought them in conflict with 'Alī, who defeated them in 658 in the battle at Al-Nahrawān. This only radicalized the situation and they planned to eliminate both 'Alī and Mu'āwiyah. The attempt to eliminate Mu'āwiyah failed, but once again, as 'Alī stood up to lead the prayers, he was struck a fatal blow on the head with a sword.

This happened in 661. We need to pause there to take note of the fact that all the Caliphs who had ruled so far had been Companions of the Prophet. This period is

---

4. Mahmoud M. Ayoub, op. cit., p. 390.

considered normative by the Sunnīs as the period of the "rightly guided" Caliphs. It will be recalled that two rival parties had emerged after the death of 'Uthmān, those who supported the call for 'Uthmān's revenge and those who supported 'Alī. Those who belonged to the party of 'Alī came to be known as *shī'ah;* the word literally meaning party. Thus arose the schism in Islam between the Sunnīs and the Shī'īs; the historical roots of this division go back to the question of succession, which the Shī'īs believe should have been 'Alī's in the first place. Hence they reject the legitimacy of the first three Caliphs.

The period of the "rightly guided Caliphs" was followed by the rule of the Umayyad dynasty in Damascus, which now became the capital. It involved the kind of change in style of governance which marked the transition of the Congress party as one opposed to British rule in India to one which supplanted it. The exchanges between Mahatma Gandhi and Pandit Nehru on this are reminiscent of the following anecdote:

> 'Umar, who had lived a simple and even austere life in Medina, is said to have reproached Mu'āwiyah as he observed the latter's great pomp and ceremony, "Is this a Persian imperial state, O Mu'āwiyah?" Mu'āwiyah justified his style of life on the ground that were he to live as 'Umar had done in Medina, no one would respect his authority.[5]

By the time this phase of the Caliphate came to an end, Islam had become a global force and presence. Huston Smith writes:

---

5. Mahmoud M. Ayoub, op. cit., p. 392.

> Two years later, in AD 632 (10 AH, After the *Hijra*), Muhammad died with virtually all of Arabia under his control. With all the power of armies and police, no other Arab had ever succeeded in uniting his countrymen as he had. Before the century closed his followers had conquered Armenia, Persia, Syria, Palestine, Iraq, North Africa, and Spain, and had crossed the Pyrenees into France. But for their defeat by Charles Martel in the Battle of Tours in 733, the entire Western world might today be Muslim. Within a brief span of mortal life, Muhammad had called forth out of unpromising material a nation never united before, in a country that was hitherto but a geographical expression; established a religion which in vast areas superseded Christianity and Judaism and still claims the adherence of a goodly portion of the human race; and laid the basis of an empire that was soon to embrace within its far-flung boundaries the fairest provinces of the then civilized world.
>
> In *The 100: A Ranking of the Most Influential Persons in History*, Michael Hart places Muhammad first. His "unparalleled combination of secular and religious influence entitles Muhammad to be considered the most influential single figure in human history," Hart writes. The explanation that Muslims give for that verdict is simple. The entire work, they say, was the work of God.[6]

The Umayyad Caliphs ruled from 661-750 over a huge empire. One incident which occurred during this period is of special significance in Islam. 'Alī had two sons — Ḥasan

6. Huston Smith, op. cit., pp. 230-31, emphasis added.

and Ḥusayn. Ḥasan had acquiesced in the take-over of the caliphate by Mu'āwiyah, but when he died his brother Ḥusayn led a revolt against the Umayyads, which produced a tragic outcome. He was defeated at Karbalā' by Yazīd, the son of Mu'āwiyah, who succeeded him. The small force of Ḥusayn was massacred, who was killed along with it. "His women and the only surviving son of 'Alī, known as Zayn Al-'Abidīn (the most excellent of all worshippers) were carried as captives, along with the heads of Ḥusayn and his fellow martyrs, first to Kūfah and from there to Yazīd in Damascus."[7] Mahmoud M. Ayoub assesses the significance of this event as follows:

> The tragedy of Karbalā has had far-reaching ramifications for Muslim faith, thought, and history. It provided an ethos of suffering and martyrdom characteristic particularly of Shī'ī faith and piety . . . but it has had a deep influence on general Sunnī piety as well. Ḥusayn's martyrdom drew for Muslims a clear distinction between the ideal Islamic polity and what was henceforth considered to be irreligious monarchial rule.[8]

In the meantime, the sentiment that someone from the Prophet's family should rule the world of Islam had not perished and accounts for the rise of the 'Abbāsid dynasty. The dynasty derives its name from Al-'Abbās, the Prophet's uncle. It ruled from 750 until 1258 from Baghdad, the city founded by the real founder of the dynasty, Al-Manṣūr (r. 754-75). In a sense it marked the apogee of Islamic power as evoked in the splendour of the tales of the *Arabian Nights*.

7. Huston Smith, op. cit., p. 394.

8. Ibid., p. 394.

The empire was destroyed by the Mongols, when they sacked Baghdad in 1258, but in what has been described as the second miracle of the Prophet — the first being the Qur'ān — the Mongols themselves converted to Islam. Thereafter different Islamic empires flourished in different parts of the world, a precedent already set by the Umayyad prince who made good his escape, when 'Abbāsids took over, to Spain and founded an Umayyad state there. The 'Abbāsids themselves were replaced by the Mamelukan Turks, who ruled from Egypt. All this while Islam was spreading in Africa and South and South-East Asia. By the time we reach the eve of modern times, the three major empires in the world (apart from the Chinese) were Muslim: the Ottoman Empire in Turkey; the Sefervid Empire in Iran, and the Mughal Empire in India.

It is important to realize that this steady expansion of Islam, through the centuries, seemed like a validation of Islam's claim to being the final revelation.

The following passage presents a concise account of such expansion.

> The religion of Islam was spread by the conquests of the Arabs in the seventh century AD over Western Asia and North Africa, and in the eighth century AD into Central Asia, Sind and Spain. Form the eleventh century AD, under Turkish leadership, it spread into Southern Russia, India and Asia Minor, and under negro leadership in the Niger basin. In the fourteenth century AD it became politically dominant in the Balkans under the Ottoman Turkish Sultans, and in India under the Sultans of Delhi; and spread, largely by missionary endeavour, into Indonesia and China.

> On the other hand, it was receding in Spain, whence it was finally expelled at the end of the fifteenth century AD. In the nineteenth and twentieth centuries AD it has lost ground in the Balkans, where it survives only in local communities (especially in Bosnia and Albania), but continues to advance in East and West Africa, and is represented by groups of immigrants in South Africa and in North and South America.[9]

It only seemed a matter of time that the whole world would come to embrace Islam, and Islam the whole world.

One can form some idea of the forces underlying the present tension between the Islamic world and the Western world from the fact that the Christian West interrupted this forward movement of Islam, and in Spain actually reversed it. This tension is beautifully reflected in two poems of Muhammad Iqbal (1877-1938), entitled *Shikwā* (Complaint) and *Jawāb-i-Shikwā* (The Answer to the Complaint), written in 1911. The year is important. Events which occurred around this time raised tension to a critical point. By then

> Iqbal and his compatriots were becoming increasingly worried about the intentions of European imperialists to take over the entire Islamic world. When the Italians invaded Tripoli in North Africa, Iqbal gave voice to the anger of his people. At the same time, the Balkan wars were taking place, wars that the Muslims understood as pressure against the Ottoman Empire. In addition, the British government had revoked the

9. H.A.R. Gibb, "Islam", in R.C. Zaehner, ed., *The Concise Encyclopedia of Living Faiths* (Boston: Beacon Press, 1967), p. 178.

> partition of Bengal, a decision that was perceived by Indian Muslims as a threat to their hopes for cultural autonomy. It looked as though Islamic civilization everywhere was on the brink of extermination.[10]

Shiela McDonough does a fine job of summarizing the contents of the two poems as follows:

> *Shikwā* is a kind of scream addressed to God from the Muslim community as they see themselves about to disintegrate and disappear from history. This loud voice shouting at the doors of heaven demands to know how God could abandon a people whose lives for centuries have been shaped by prayer, fasting, and service to the commands of the one God. The accusation is that God is deserting the very people who have been most faithful to Him.
>
> The poem was greeted with much enthusiasm when it was recited in Lahore. The people's love for Iqbal's poetry increased because he so vividly articulated their confusion and despair. But, typically, Iqbal having made a strong statement, looks at the issue from another perspective, and writes his version of how God responds to the complaint from the Muslims. This is *Jawāb-i-Shikwā* (The Answer to the Complaint). The people have made so much noise that God has to recognize them.
>
> The answer is that the failure lies with the Muslims, and not with God, who remains the same, Just, Good and Transcendent. The people have not understood

---

10. Sheila McDonough, *The Flame of Sinai: Hope and Vision in Iqbal* (Lahore: Iqbal Academy, Pakistan, 2002), p. 71.

what was expected of them. Iqbal wrote this at a time when the European powers were dominant over Muslims everywhere. It may well have seemed to many that Muslim independence was about to disappear forever. The answer to the complaint is that God remains God, no matter what happens in history. The problem for humans in any time and place is to grasp the judgement of God upon their immediate situation, and to try to see what that judgment tells them they should do. The reply is a rejection of mourning over the loss of the past. Believers are told always to look forward. The answer says: God does not accept self-pity; He demands transformation.[11]

11. Sheila McDonough, op. cit., pp. 71-72.

7

Islamic Mysticism

THE account of Islam in terms of its legal structure and historical spread may leave the Hindu reader with the impression that Islam is a very political, legal and this-worldly religion. It certainly possesses these dimensions. Most of the major religions of the world do. But no account of any of these religions could be considered complete without alluding to their mystical dimension.

Islam possesses this dimension in ample measure and it is referred to as Sufism. The word *ṣūfī* refers to a person who wears patched woolen garments, probably as a symbolic rejection of ostentatious living in favour of one devoted to God. The historical expansion and material enrichment of Islam, it has been argued, was felt by at least some if not many as a move away from the true spirit of Islam, and Sufism represented a protest against this trend. The fact that the first phase in the history of Sufism is marked by a strong ascetic streak lends some credence to this view. It should not be imagined however that the roots of Islamic mysticism cannot be traced back to the Qur'ān and indeed to the Prophet's own example. The following verses of the Qur'ān are often cited lest the mystical dimension of the text be overlooked: In one verse of the Qur'ān, God is said to be closer to a human being "than his own jugular vein" (50:16). God also says: "I am near to answer the call of the caller when he calls to me" (2.182). Ṣūfīs have also been inclined to think that the following fragment of the Qur'ān has a special implication for them: "Those whom God loves and who love him (5: 54)."

Asceticism, combined with a fear of God's judgement, was a major feature in the early phase of Sufism. Al-Ḥasan (642-728) of Basra, who undertook the Ḥajj on foot three times, incarnates this attitude. Gradually, however, this fear of God was replaced by the love of God, a transition in which the woman mystic called Rābi'ah (*c*. 713-801) (who may remind some Hindu readers of Mīrā) plays a role. When people sought her hand in marriage this is how she dealt with the situation.

> The Ṣūfīs of Basra urged Rābi'a to choose a husband from among them, rather than continue to live unmarried. She replied, "Willingly," and asked which of them was most religious. They replied that it was Ḥasan. So she said to him that if he could give her the answer to four questions, she would become his wife.
>
> "What will the Judge of the world say when I die? That I have come forth from the world a Muslim, or an unbeliever?"
>
> Ḥasan answered, "This is among the hidden things known only to God . . .."
>
> Then she said, "When I am put in the grave and Munkar and Nakīr (the angels who question the dead) question me, shall I be able to answer them (satisfactorily) or not?" He replied, "This is also hidden."

> "When people are assembled at the Resurrection and the books are distributed, shall I be given mine in my right hand or my left?" . . . "This also is among the hidden things."
>
> Finally she asked, "When mankind is summoned (at the Judgment), some to Paradise and some to Hell, in which group shall I be?" He answered, "This too is hidden, and none knows what is hidden save God — His is the glory and the majesty."
>
> Then she said to him, "Since this is so, and I have these four questions with which to concern myself, how should I need a husband, with whom to be occupied?" (She remained unmarried.)[1]

According to legend she was sometimes seen moving about with a pail of water and a torch. The pail of water was meant to put out the fires of hell and the torch was meant to set heaven on fire. The account appears less quixotic if we take the following famous statement of hers into account: "O God! If I worship thee in fear of hell, burn me in hell; and if I worship thee in hope of paradise, exclude me from paradise; but if I worship thee for thine own sake then withhold not thine everlasting beauty."[2]

A third aspect in the development of Sufism focused on the knowledge of God.

Sufism speaks of a unitive vision of God, which bears some striking resemblances to the accounts found in Hindu

1. See Mahmoud M. Ayoub, op. cit., pp. 430-31.
2. Reynold A. Nicholson, *The Mystics of Islam*, Harmondsworth: Penguin Books, 1989 (1914) p. 115.

literature. Bābā Kūhi of Shīraz, who died in CE 1050, wrote:

In the market, in the cloister — only God I saw.
In the valley and on the mountain — only God I saw.
Him I have seen beside me oft in tribulation;
In favour and in fortune — only God I saw.
In prayer and fasting, in praise and contemplation,
In the religion of the Prophet — only God I saw.
Neither soul nor body, accident nor substance,
Qualities nor causes — only God I saw.
I opened mine eyes and by the light of His face around me
In all the eye discovered — only God I saw.
Like a candle I was melting in his fire:
Amidst the flames outflashing — only God I saw.
Myself with mine own eyes I saw most clearly,
But when I looked with God's eyes — only God I saw.
I passed away into nothingness, I vanished,
And lo, I was the All-living — only God I saw.[3]

A mystic whom Hindus might find particularly intriguing is Al-Ḥallāj (*c.* 852-922), who is also said to have travelled to India. He was initiated into Sufism early in his life and studied with the best known mystic masters of his time, including al-Junayd.

> After some time, al-Hallāj broke away form his teachers and embarked on the long and dangerous quest of self-realization. It all began when he went one day to see al-Junayd, who asked who was at the door, and al-Hallāj answered, "I, the absolute divine truth" (*anā al-Ḥaqq*). *Al-Ḥaqq* is one of the ninety-nine "wonderful names" of God mentioned in the *Qur'ān*.

3. Reynold A. Nicholson, op. cit., p. 59.

> Al-Junayd is reported to have sharply reprimanded his wayward disciple and predicted an evil end for him.[4]

Al-Ḥallāj was executed for his extraordinary claim, which flies in the face of Islamic orthodoxy but comes close to being virtually synonymous with the *mahāvākya*: *aham brahmāsmi*.

It is interesting to see how the later mystic tradition tried to defend him. Three attempts to exonerate him of the charge of blasphemy are particularly interesting. (1) According to one view, Ḥallāj went against the Law and had to be executed for it, but not because he went against the truth.[5] (2) According to another view, Ḥallāj got carried away. Rūmī provides an example: just as a piece of red-hot coal in a furnace might begin to think that it is fire, Ḥallāj was in a state of such deep union with God that he thought he was God himself and made the statement in such a condition. (3) According to yet another view, when Ḥallāj cried *anā al-ḥaqq* "it was not Hallāj who cried *'Ana 'l-Haqq'* but God himself, speaking, as it were, by the mouth of the selfless Hallāj, just as he spoke to Moses through the medium of the burning bush (Kor. 20.8-14)."[6]

One of the most famous poet-saints or poet-mystics in Islam is Jalāl al-Dīn Rūmī (1207-73), whose famous book *Mathnawi* (Couplets) has been described as the Qur'ān in Persian. A well-known poem of his seems to combine the

---

4. Mahmoud M. Ayoub, op. cit., p. 434.
5. Reynold A. Nicholson, op. cit., p. 152.
6. Ibid.

ideas of "evolution" and "reincarnation" and *mokṣa,* which imparts to it a unique flavour:

I died as mineral and became a plant,
I died as plant and rose to animal,
I died as animal and I was man.
Why should I fear? When was I less by dying?
Yet once more I shall die as man, to soar
With angels blest; but even from angelhood
I must pass on: all except God doth perish.
When I have sacrificed my angel soul,
I shall become what no mind e'er conceived.
Oh, let me not exist! for Non-existence
Proclaims in organ tones, "To him we shall return."[7]

The sheer lyrical power of Rūmī's mystical poetry is such that it comes through even in translations.

Happy the moment when we are seated in the Palace, thou and I,
With two forms and with two figures but with one soul, thou and I.
The colours of the grove and the voice of the birds will bestow immortality
At the time when we come into the garden, thou and I.
The stars of heaven will come to gaze upon us;
We shall show them the Moon itself, thou and I.
Thou and I, individuals no more, shall be mingled in ecstasy,
Joyful and secure from foolish babble, thou and I.

---

7. Reynold A. Nicholson, op. cit., p. 168.

> *All the bright-plumed birds of heaven will devour their hearts with envy*
> *In the place where we shall laugh in such a fashion, thou and I.*
> *This is the greatest wonder, that thou and I, sitting here in the same nook,*
> *Are at this moment both in Irāq and Khorāsān, thou and I.*[8]

Sufism in full bloom was sometimes characterised by an attitude towards other religions usually associated with Hinduism. Ibn 'Arabī (1165-1240), known as the Great *Shaykh* or Master, declared: "My heart has become capable of every form, a pasture for gazelles, a cloister for monks, a temple for idols, the votary's Ka'bah, the tablets of the Torah, the surah of the Qur'ān. It is the religion of love that I hold: wherever turns its mounts, love shall be my religion and my faith."[9]

The pre-modern Islamic world was an arabesque of *ṣūfī* orders called *silasila*s which crisscrossed it. Purist trends in modern Islam, however, tend to blame Sufism for the decline of Islam in the face of the rise of the West.

---

8. Reynold A. Nicholson, op. cit., pp. 167-68.
9. Mahmood M. Ayoub, op. cit., p. 438.

8

Can Muslims Talk to Hindus?

I

A QUESTION such as the one being raised here, namely: Can Muslims talk to Hindus? — can be addressed at several levels. One could, for instance, ask what kind of a Muslim are we talking about: an "orthodox" Muslim; a Ṣūfī Muslim or "folk"-Muslim, by which I mean a Muslim sharing a folk-culture with the Hindus. Even these three levels are capable of further subdivision. The categories are admittedly loose and may overlap. It is virtually impossible to do justice to all these levels. Hence in this chapter we shall avail only of the category we may call "orthodox" Islam. Far be it from me however to try to determine what is orthodox in Islam. What I shall do is to look at the Qur'ān, as a text which is bound to figure in any definition of Islamic orthodoxy, and ask of it the question: Can Muslims talk to Hindus according to the Qur'ān and if so on what basis? I shall also avoid taking the most obvious route and ask if Hindus are a "People of the Book" like the Jews and Christians, as a basis for engaging in dialogue with Muslims, partly from the realization that, as I look around, the three "people" with the Book hardly seem to be on talking-terms with each other in many parts of the world. So if we want the Muslims to talk to the Hindus we may wish to find another way.

I shall now present three arguments, in the hope that each will reveal progressively unambiguous grounds for Muslims and Hindus to talk to each other.

II

According to the Qur'ān (35.23; 57.25) prophets have been sent to all the peoples of the world. And according to the same Qur'ān — and this is crucial — believing Muslims should make no distinctions among the prophets (II.136) but treat them all on par. Obviously then Muslims can not only talk to Hindus but do so on the basis of equality rather than on the basis of treating them either as a "protected people" or "people with a Book" in the conventional sense. Lest the reader feel that one is being too innovative in proposing this position, permit me to cite Prof. Fazlur Rahman on this point. He writes:

> There is no mention of any fixed religious communities in the earlier part of the Qur'ān. True, different prophets have come to different peoples and nations at different times, but their messages are universal and identical. All these messages emanate from a single source: "the Mother of the Book" (43, 4; 13, 39) and "the Hidden Book" (56:78). Since these messages are universal and identical, it is incumbent on all people to believe in all divine messages. This is why Muḥammad felt himself obligated to believe in the prophethood of Noah, Abraham, Moses, and Jesus, for God's religion is indivisible and prophethood is also indivisible. Indeed, the Prophet is made to declare

> in the Qur'ān that not only does he believe in the Torah and the Gospel but "I believe in whatever Book God may have revealed" (42:15). This is because God's guidance is universal and not restricted to any nation or nations: "And there is no nation wherein a warner has not come" (35:24) and "For every people a guide has been provided" (13:7). The word "Book" is, in fact, often used in the Qur'ān not with reference to any specific revealed book but as a generic term denoting the totality of divine revelations (see 2:213, for example).[1]

This promising passage however also poses a problem. While the conclusion one would be tempted to draw from such a passage is that Muslims, if they believe in Prophet Muḥammad, must equally believe in the other prophets, Professor Fazlur Rahman, to whom I must ultimately defer, moves the interpretation in the opposite direction and goes on to say: "If Muḥammad and his followers believe in all prophets, all people must also and equally believe in him. Disbelief in him would be equivalent to disbelief in all, for this would arbitrarily upset the line of prophetic succession."[2] The promise of the passage from our point of view is only partially realized when it is interpreted this way.

Its potential in our context is also compromised in another way. Although according to the Qur'ān prophets were sent to all the peoples, the names of all of them are

---

1. Fazlur Rahman, *Major Themes of the Qur'ān* (Minneapolis: Bibliotheca Islamica, 1980), pp. 163-64.
2. Ibid., p. 164.

not mentioned in the Qur'ān (IV.164; II.106; XIII.39). A number of them are mentioned but the list of prophets actually mentioned in the Qur'ān is self-admittedly not exhaustive. This creates an ambiguity in relation to the Hindus, for neither they nor their scriptures or prophets find *explicit* mention in the Qur'ān. The ambiguity may be stated as follows: because they are *not* mentioned in the Qur'ān one cannot *categorically* claim that prophets are found among them, but because the enumeration of the prophets in the Qur'ān is not exhaustive, the possibility cannot be denied either. One can neither assert nor deny the point in relation to the Hindus.

Such ambiguity also compromises this line of argument.

III

There is however another passage in the Qur'ān which seems to provide a more solid basis for a Muslim to talk to a Hindu. A verse (V.48) in the fifth *Sūrah* of the Qur'ān runs as follows in the translation offered by Martin Lings:

> *For each of you we have appointed a law and a way.*
> *And if God had willed He would have made you one people.*
> *But He has willed it otherwise in that He may put you to the test in what He has given to you.*
> *So vie with one another in good works.*
> *Unto God will ye be brought back,*
> *And He will inform you about that wherein ye differed.*[3]

3. Seyyed Hossein Nasr, "Religion, Globality, and Universality", in Arvind Sharma and Kathleen Dugan, eds., *A Dome of Many Colors: Studies in Religious Pluralism, Identity and Unity* (Harrisburg, Pennsylvania: Trinity Press International, 1999), p. 154.

This verse has the merit of putting metaphysical or eschatological issues on hold, as it were, among the various religious communities. And it also alludes to the people being judged by the revelation received *by* them. This creates more room for dialogue. Professor Fazlur Rahman identifies this verse of the Qur'ān as the Qur'ān's "final answer to the problem of a multi-community world."[4] Professor Seyyed Hossein Nasr also seems to share this view.

This verse however also involves the fact of each community having received a revelation, which is mediated through the prophets. And we saw earlier that some doubt in this respect *could* be raised in relation to Hinduism. This verse also does not throw open the door for a dialogue between the Muslim and the Hindu, although conceivably the door could be opened — though not without some creaking — depending on how liberal a view one is prepared to entertain in this context.

IV

I would now like to discuss a third option provided by Verse 13 of *Sūrah* 49 which runs as follows in the translation by Pickthall:

> O mankind! Lo! We have created you male and female, and we have made you nations and tribes that ye may know one another. Lo! The noblest of you in the sight of Allah, is the best in conduct. Lo! Allah is Knower, Aware.[5]

---

4. Fazlur Rahman, op. cit., p. 167.
5. Mohammed Marmaduke Pickthall, *The Meaning of the Glorious Koran* (New York: The New American Library, 1972), p. 369.

This verse seems to offer the clearest mandate for the Muslim to talk to the Hindu. The verse, a Medina verse, is addressed specifically to humanity, not just Muslims and in this verse the diversity not just of peoples but of sexes is clearly alluded to. Note that no revelations have been sent in terms of the division of humanity by sex, but rather to the peoples. Not only is the diversity of the peoples alluded to, there are no qualifications attached to it, such that they be Jews or Christians or Sabeans. Moreover, the purpose of this diversity is also identified. It is to provide an occasion for the people to know each other — or to put it in modern idiom — engage in dialogue, so that it might bring out the best in them. Hence Muslims and Hindus can talk to each other not (only) because revelation is universal but because *diversity is universal* — a pervasive feature of the human condition. In other words, the diversity being celebrated here is "radical," in its etymological sense of pertaining to the roots and as providing a root metaphor of the human condition.

I would therefore propose that it is possible for the Muslims to talk to the Hindus, without this possibility having to be mediated through the category of *ahl al-kitāb*; which is to say that Muslims can talk directly to the Hindus just because they constitute two distinct communities and that this difference is meant to enable them to come to know each other. The Qur'ān provides what we might call an anthropological basis here, as distinguished from a revelatory basis, for the Muslims to talk to the Hindus.[6]

6. That "ethnic and cultural diversity are part of God's plan, as the Qur'ān confirms (49:13)" was a fact accepted by Ibn Taymiyya (d. 1328), see Tamara Sonn, *A Brief History of Islam* (Malden, MA: Blackwell Publishing, 2004), p. 127. The verse however is cited here in the context of *internal* diversity within Islam. For Muslim views of Hinduism in India see Yohanan Friedmann, "Medieval Muslim views of Indian Religions", *Journal of the American Oriental Society,* vol. 5, no. 2 (April–June 1975) pp. 214-21.

Bibliography

Arberry, Arthur J., *The Koran Interpreted*, New York: The Macmillan Company, 1955.

Ayoub, Mahmoud M., "The Islamic Tradition", in Willard G. Oxtoby, ed., *World Religions: Western Traditions*, Toronto: Oxford University Press, 1996.

Burke, Patrick, *The Major Religions: An Introduction with Texts*, Malden, MA: Blackwell Publishing, 2004.

Byrant, Edwin, *The Quest for the Origins of Vedic Culture: The Indo-Aryan Migration Debate*, New York: Oxford University Press, 2001.

Davies, J.G., "Christianity: The Early Church", in R.C. Zaehner, ed., *The Concise Encyclopedia of Living Faiths*, Boston: Beacon Press, 1967.

Deutsch, Eliot and Rohit Dalvi, *The Essential Vedānta: A New Source Book of Advaita Vedānta*, Bloomignton, Indiana: World Wisdom Inc., 2004.

Fisher, Mary Pat, *Living Religions*, 5th edn., Upper Saddle River, N.J.: Prentice-Hall, 2002.

Friedmann, Yohanan, "Medieval Views of Indian Religion", *Journal of the American Oriental Society*, vol. 5, no. 2 (April–June, 1975), pp. 214-221.

Gibb, H.A.R., "Islam", in R.C. Zaehner, ed., *The Concise Encyclopedia of Living Faiths*, Boston: Beacon Press, 1967.

Guillaume, A., *The Life of Muhammad: A Translation of Ishaq's sīrat rasūl allāh*, Karachi: Oxford University Press, 1980 [1955].

Hiriyanna, M., *Popular Essays in Indian Philosophy*, Mysore: Kavyalaya

Publishers, 1952.

Mahadevan, T.M.P., *Outlines of Hinduism*, Bombay: Chetana Limited, 1971.

McDonough, Sheila, *The Flame of Sinai: Hope and Vision in Iqbal*, Lahore: Iqbal Academy Pakistan, 2002.

Nasr, Seyyed Hossein, "Islam", in Arvind Sharma, ed., *Our Religions*, San Francisco: Harper Collins, 1993.

———, "Religion, Globality, and Universality", in Arvind Sharma and Kathleen Dugan, eds., *A Dome of Many Colors: Studies in Religious Pluralism, Identity and Unity*, Harrisburg, Pennsylvania: Trinity Press International, 1999.

Nicholson, Reynold A., *The Mystics of Islam*, Harmondsworth: Penguin Books, 1989 [1914].

Oxtoby, Willard G., ed., *World Religions: Western Traditions*, Toronto: Oxford University Press, 1996.

Pickthall, Mohammed Marmaduke, tr., *The Meaning of the Glorious Koran*, New York: The New American Library, 1972.

Rahman, Fazlur, *Major Themes of the Qur'ān*, Minneapolis: Bibliotheca Islamica, 1980.

Radhakrishnan, S., ed., *The Principal Upaniṣads*, Atlantic Heights, NJ: Humanities Press International, Inc., 1992 [1953].

Sharma, Arvind, ed., *Our Religions*, San Francisco: Harper Collins, 1993.

——— and Kathleen Dugan, eds., *A Dome of Many Colors: Studies in Religious Pluralism, Identity and Unity*, Harrisburg, Pennsylvania: Trinity Press International, 1999.

Smith, Huston, *The World's Religions*, San Francisco: Harper Collins, 1991.

Sonn, Tamara, *A Brief History of Islam*, Malden, MA: Blackwell Publishing, 2004.

Zaehner, R.C., ed., *The Concise Encyclopedia of Living Faiths*, Boston: Beacon Press, 1967.

Index